THE

LAROUSSE

BOOK OF

BREAD

THE
LAROUSSE
BOOK OF
BREAD

RECIPES
TO MAKE AT HOME

ÉRIC KAYSER

FOREWORD

Around the late nineties, the French rediscovered bread—not just any old bread, but the bread that, these days, is offered by exceptional artisan bakers. The use of natural leavens and quality flours, the alliance of tradition and technology, the inventiveness—these are some of the reasons for the renaissance. Tired of soulless commercial products, consumers now want to understand how their bread is made, and this book is a response to those demands.

It is a short journey from the quest for good bread to making it yourself, and renowned French artisan baker Éric Kayser wants you to take that step. His goal for you is ambitious because he invites you to throw yourself into the process of making bread using natural leaven. You will easily find the ingredients you need for the recipes in this book in good supermarkets and specialist stores. You already have an oven. If you don't want to knead by hand you can use an electric stand mixer. If you work with good ingredients, you are already more than halfway there. For the rest, there are the step-by-step explanations of the recipes, which you can follow in Massimo Pessina's close-up photographs.

Éric Kayser, who runs many bakeries in France and abroad, receives a constant stream of requests from private individuals who want to spend a night in the bakery, baking bread. This book demonstrates his eagerness to satisfy the urge that many of us have to touch and feel dough with our own hands and, through making it ourselves, to understand what bread really is. "People today are seeking authenticity in all kinds of things," he explains. "And what could be better than bread, when it is made honestly, with no trickery or artifice, to convey this feeling of authenticity?"

FOR THE LOVE OF BREAD

I come from a long line of bakers originating in Alsace in France. My family is from the Franche-Comté, specifically from a town called Lure, where my father practiced the craft and passed it to me. As a child, I loved the time that I spent with him in the bakery and I always saw myself following in his footsteps—but in a different way, somehow combining the job with my childhood dreams of traveling the world. Although my father was happy in his work, I had the impression that he was tied to his bakery. The image of the artisan baker, working seven days a week and part of the nights, will either entice or deter you. I persisted, starting an apprenticeship in Fréjus, at Gérard Levant's bakery. There I learned how to mix the dough, how to make the leaven, how to put bread in the oven with a baker's peel. Levant was a good teacher who passed on to me the love of work well done. At that time, there were no restrictions on working hours for minors, and I often started before 1 A.M. One time, I took a girl out to go dancing and explained that I would disappear by midnight, like Cinderella. When she asked why, I told her that I was a baker... and the spell was broken. But while these can be the drawbacks of the occupation, they did not discourage me.

While doing my military service I took the opportunity of signing up as a conscript in Lebanon, where I joined the blue berets of the UNFIL (United Nations Interim Force in Lebanon). That experience only reaffirmed my desire to see the world. On returning to France, I joined the *Compagnons du Devoir* ("Companions of Duty"), a workers' association that offered apprentices opportunities to further their training and to travel. The chance to gain practical knowledge while traveling appealed to me. Collective life had many rules. My daily routine comprised a total of 10 hours of work, on top of which I had 5-6 hours of lessons—either giving or receiving them—as well as various tasks and duties to carry out within the community. I completed my "Tour of France" in four years, earning on graduation the name *Franc-Comtois le Décidé* ("The resolute Franc-Comtois").

Living with others, sharing, receiving, giving: these are the values most at risk in young people, who often prefer to shut themselves in their rooms playing video games. I learned from the *Compagnons* the desire to do good, as well as tenacity and a love of honest work. My own experiences instilled in me a desire to help prevent apprentices going astray in the world, to teach them how to respect others and to earn respect themselves. I believe in humankind. Within every lost soul, there is always something good that will help him find his way, provided he allows himself to be helped. I am absolutely delighted that the *Compagnons du Devoir* is now open to women, which was not the case in my day. Some of them have become remarkable stonemasons or bakers.

At the request of the Companionship, I was asked to help develop training programs for the future. At the time, I was already running training courses and work-placement schemes for the *Institut National de la Boulangerie Pâtisserie* (the INBP, or the National Institute of Baking and Pastry-Making—France's leading technical college for bakers). These internships operated within the framework of the *Centres de Formation d'Apprentis* (CFA, or Centers for the Training of Apprentices) and then shifted to bakeries. Over the course of two to three nights, we would show bakers how to organize their work. It was a question of not hurting people's feelings and I found the experience character-building. In the course of these training sessions Patrick Castagna (a greatly valued trainer by INBP) and I began to realize that bakers who had abandoned natural leavens after the war wanted to go back to using them, but did not know how. So together, in 1992, we created a baking consultancy (Panis Victor) and started to develop a concept for a machine that would be capable of handling natural leavens. The gradual adoption of natural leavens by French bakers meant that millers were starting to offer us bakers ancient varieties of high-quality wheat flour that had been abandoned because of low yields. The entire industry, from field to bakery, began to be questioned. We developed the concept for our Fermentolevain machine in association with the bakery division of the Swedish company Electrolux. It meant a great deal of traveling around the world to launch our machines. Fermentolevain won the Innovation Award at Europain 1994.

On 13 September, 1996, I opened my first bread shop at 8 rue Monge in Paris—partly inspired by memories of my father's bakery. I wanted to reproduce a child's picture book image of the traditional bakery, complete with a bread oven built on a hearth of firebricks. We were resolved to banish people's vision of dreary supermarket shelves with their limp plastic-wrapped baguettes. There is little doubt that the use of quality flours and natural leavens, together with skilled kneading and baking, have all contributed to French people's renewed desire for bread with complex aromas and a fresh, light crumb. These days, I fly around the world to open new bakeries on other continents and to bring a love of French bread to people who have never tasted it. But I do miss the hands-on contact with dough, and I often feel the urge to return to a bakery and to start kneading.

— Éric Kayser

THE BASICS OF BREAD MAKING

FLOURS

It is possible to make excellent bread with all types of flours, provided the raw materials are of good quality. If you love bread and enjoy making it, you will be tempted to try out different kinds of flour. To familiarize yourself with the experience of bread making, I advise you to begin with all-purpose (plain) flour.

To make the recipes more accessible to readers worldwide, I have provided recommendations for flours which are more readily available outside of France. French flours require less water to produce dough of the same consistency as American flours, and as flours can behave differently, I strongly advise using the flours suggested to ensure good results. If you prefer to bake with the original French flours, see the flour conversions on page 305.

ANCIENT AND MODERN FLOURS

The quality of bread depends, above all, on the quality of the ingredients and then on the way they are put to work. The crises that have shaken the food-processing industry mean that it's important to be vigilant. Ever since World War II, industrial wheat production has been dominated by the profit imperative, not by quality and nutritional concerns. This meant that high-yielding types of wheat won out and, as a consequence, during the 1970s–80s, bread had very little flavor. Eventually, however, increasing concerns led to a reassessment of the wheat-flour-bread sector.

Nowadays, millers are producing flours made from formerly cultivated ancient wheat varieties that had been abandoned because of low yields. These flours are more strongly pigmented and provide exceptional nutritional value as well as pleasing colors and flavors of both crumb and crust. They form a protein chain that can contain gassy pressure without resulting in rubbery dough. The quality of the proteins is the determining factor rather than the percentage (around 10–12%). My millers work with farmers who have adopted the French CRC standard (*Culture Raisonnée et Controlée*) of "rational and controlled agriculture."

USING ORGANIC FLOURS

There was a time when I preferred to use organic flours, but the prohibitive costs were putting customers off. Additionally, while organic farming by definition excludes pesticides and insecticides, there is always the possibility of contamination from adjoining areas which are being cultivated to different standards. Rational and controlled agriculture (CRC) has the advantages of organic cultivation without the inconveniences. It is called "rational" because it ensures the use of good quality raw materials as well as methods of production which respect the environment. In the end, it's a question of judgment: of avoiding the most harmful insecticides and pesticides, without eliminating them altogether, and of accepting a lower yield per acre. This method is less rigid and, in a way, more realistic.

CHOICE OF FLOURS

If you settle for the first bag of flour you see in the supermarket, you will have great difficulty in making good bread. All-purpose (plain) flour is usually a T65 type, which is a lower protein flour, derived from wheat that has been cultivated using pesticides and insecticides and "corrected" with ascorbic acid, added gluten, and permitted additives.

Read the label carefully before buying: the presence of enzymes to facilitate better fermentation is acceptable, but nothing else. The advantage of using a rationally-farmed flour is that you get precise information and genuine traceability. You know what ingredients you are mixing, and what you will eat as a result.

ASH CONTENT

Millers assess the quality of flour by the quantity of mineral-rich husks (the external covering of the grain, also called bran) that are present. To determine the ratio of minerals present, a small amount of flour is incinerated at 1652°F (900°C). Being non-combustible, the remaining minerals or "ash" determine the type of flour. Broadly, higher-protein flours have a higher ash content. This measure is used in France to give flour a "T" grade. T65, or all-purpose (plain) flour, which is what I recommend (unless indicated otherwise), has an ash content of 0.62-0.75%.

Unbleached flours are increasingly sought-after, where the ash content is 0.75% or higher (Types 80, 110, or 150). The more complete the flour, the more it will have retained husks that have been in contact with pesticides and insecticides. Stick to organic or CRC suppliers for this kind of flour. In general, "type" is associated with wheat flour (or froment), but the same categories exist for other cereals such as spelt flour, einkorn (or small spelt), and rye flour.

If you prefer cereals such as spelt or einkorn, which are ancestors of modern-day wheat, be aware that the dough will require your full attention, as the gluten networks of these flours are more fragile. I recommend that you use the suggested flours to ensure good results.

COMPOSITION
OF A GRAIN OF WHEAT
A grain of wheat is composed of three parts: the farinaceous kernel made up of starch and gluten (81-83% of the grain), the germ (2-3%), and the encasing husks, which are rich in fiber and minerals (14-17%). Starch, a slow-acting carbohydrate, plays an essential role in bread making, activating the yeasts that develop the dough.

Gluten, a composite pf proteins, is found in wheat, spelt, Kamut®, and einkorn, and also, in lesser proportions, in rye, oats, and barley. The presence of gluten is essential for dough that is supple and elastic, which means that the bread will acquire a light crumb. The wheat germ is rich in vitamins and minerals.

CHOOSING
THE RIGHT INGREDIENTS

The four essential ingredients in bread making are flour, the starter, salt, and water.
I would also add a fifth ingredient: passion.

LIQUID STARTER
You will see on page 25 how to make a liquid
sourdough starter and how to sustain
it by feeding or "refreshing" it. I strongly
recommend you try this technique: it is
easy, fun, and fascinating. And you will end
up with a sourdough starter that you can use
whenever you want.

DEHYDRATED STARTER
If you'd rather not make your own sourdough
starter, you can use a dehydrated version,
which is sold in organic food stores.
This starter activates on contact with water
when added to the mixing bowl with other
ingredients. However, the high baker's yeast
content in these powders will partly inhibit
the development of the starter.

FRESH BAKER'S YEAST
Available from good bread shops, specialist
food stores, or large supermarkets,
it comes in blocks or foil-wrapped cubes,
which can be sprinkled directly into the flour
and water mixture. Yeast should not come
into direct contact with salt. It should
be kept at a temperature between 32–50°F
(0–10°C). In the recipes in this book,
it complements the action of the starter but
does not replace it.

DRY YEAST
This comes in two types: active dry yeast,
which must be dissolved in lukewarm water
before use, and freeze-dried or instant
dry yeast, which is mixed directly into the
flour and water. Whichever dry yeast you use,

you'll need only half the amount of fresh
yeast indicated in the recipe.

SALT
I recommend using an unrefined salt, like
Fleur de Sel de Guérande or another artisan
sea salt equivalent—preferably with a high
iodine content. "Unrefined" means it comes
in flakes or crystals and still contains all
its minerals, such as magnesium. My
scientifically unproven conviction is that
this type of salt helps bread to keep longer.

WATER
In my bakery we use softeners to purify
tap water. In an ideal world it would be best
to use spring water, but think about how it
reaches you: in plastic bottles! I do believe
it's a good start to neutralize impurities and
limestone in the water as much as possible,
and to achieve this easily, you can use a water
filter pitcher or attach a filter to the tap.

△ While accuracy is important—and for this reason
  I weigh water rather than measuring it by
  volume—the amounts of water indicated in the
  recipes may need to be adjusted: you may need
  to reduce or increase them depending on the
  humidity, the quality of the flour, or your ability
  to knead high-hydration—wet and sticky—
  dough. Bread making is all about intuition.

OTHER INGREDIENTS
Many other ingredients can be used to make
bread—milk, olive oil, seeds, nuts, honey, dried
fruit, seaweed... Whichever you choose, always
bear in mind that poor-quality ingredients
can spoil bread made with good-quality flour.

EQUIPMENT

Launching into the adventure of bread making does not require a major investment in special equipment. If your kitchen already has a basic oven, all you have to do is ensure you have the ingredients you need before starting to mix your dough. Kneading by hand is an invaluable experience that I heartily recommend. However, if you plan to make bread frequently or if you find wet and sticky dough hard to deal with, you can use an electric mixer. Here are some tips for investing in several utensils that can make the task easier.

BAKER'S CLOTH OR COUCHE
These heavy linen cloths are useful when proofing dough or rolls. They are slightly dampened before being placed over the bowl or directly over rolls. If lightly dusted with flour, you can also use them to hold rolls in place during a second rise, or to line a small bowl or basket, thereby transforming it into a banneton. Alternatively, you could use a clean, heavyweight dish cloth.

BAKING STONE
Also called a "pizza stone," this is placed on a rack at the bottom of the oven to preheat. It absorbs the heat of the oven and transmits it to the bread placed directly on it.
You can use a little wooden paddle, or baker's peel, to place the dough on a baking stone. These are both available from specialist suppliers.

BANNETONS
These are wicker proofing baskets, lined with heavy linen, that come in different shapes and sizes. For very wet doughs, or when you are only have a single loaf to proof, a banneton may be needed for proofing. They are available from specialist food stores and suppliers.

BREAD LAMES
Specialist suppliers carry special razor-sharp blades with holders, known as *grignettes*, which are used to score or slash the dough and so control how it expands during baking.
A utility knife or a well-sharpened knife can be used instead, but it may drag across the dough or tear.

DIGITAL PROBE THERMOMETER
It will give the temperature of the dough and help you to calculate the base temperature (see page 20).

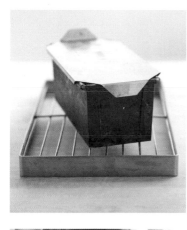

DOUGH SCRAPER

If you are kneading by hand, this is very useful for scraping the dough from the work surface. It can also be used to scrape out dough from a mixer or bowl, or for cleaning it off your fingers.

ELECTRIC STAND MIXER

There are several brands, with different-strength motors and mixing speeds. When using a stand mixer, make sure that the dough hook reaches the bottom of the bowl—otherwise, the dough may not be mixed uniformly.

MEASURING CUPS

I have included cup measurements, but I strongly advise you to invest in a scale, which can be fairly inexpensive, and measure by weights to ensure an accurate result. When measuring flour by cups, whisk the flour before measuring.

MIXING BOWL

All the recipes in this book use 500 g (scant 4 cups) of flour. If you will be mixing by hand, select a large bowl.

PANS AND MOLDS

In some instances, shaped pans or molds can be crucial in achieving the best proof and bake. Sometimes they are used to create a particular shape. For instance, when baking Pumpernickel (page 132), a long rectangular pan with a sliding lid is used to create the desired straight-edged loaf. The lid is closed during the proofing stage and while cooking. These pans are available from specialist suppliers.

STEAM

For the best results, a touch of steam is essential when the dough first goes into the oven. This can be achieved by preheating a baking sheet in the bottom of the oven and pouring in 50 g (scant ¼ cup) water just as the bread goes into the oven. Rolls can also be lightly sprayed with water before they go in the oven, or even lightly dampened by brushing with water.

VARIOUS OTHER UTENSILS

These are the little implements that complete your basic equipment: a rolling pin to stretch the dough for certain recipes; scissors to shape bread rolls; brushes to moisten or glaze bread rolls or to oil pans; a timer to indicate the rising or cooking time; a sifter (sieve) for dusting with flour; a brush for dusting off excess flour and parchment (baking) paper to avoid dirtying oven pans.

WEIGHING SCALES

When making bread I weigh all the ingredients using measuring scales—even water—as it is more accurate than using measuring cups (i.e. flours may be packed differently). You can use either digital or mechanical scales. Some digital scales will weigh to 1 g accuracy.

KNEADING

Kneading can be done either in an electric stand mixer or by hand (which will take longer). The great joy of making bread at home is the pleasure of kneading by hand, which we cannot do in commercial bakeries for reasons of hygiene. "Hands-on" kneading is a required experience for anyone who wants to learn how to make bread, because the hands receive the essential information on the progress of the dough's development.

EACH BREAD DEMANDS APPROPRIATE KNEADING

Whether you knead by hand or with a stand mixer, the recipe and the flour you use will determine the appropriate way of kneading. The quantity of water required and the kneading time vary depending on these parameters as well as on your own progress in the art of bread making.

High-hydration doughs (with a high moisture content), roughly 80% water, are wet and sticky, which makes them difficult to knead by hand. However, they result in an open, honeycombed crumb that is much enjoyed. For this type of dough, you may prefer to use a mixer. Bear in mind that in baking the recipe is merely a suggestion: you should work by following your instincts. Even if you use a stand mixer to knead the dough, you should still use your fingers to assess its texture or tackiness in order to decide the best approach to take.

BASE TEMPERATURE

This is an essential baking principle. The temperature of dough after kneading (generally 75.2-77°F [24-25°C]), depends on a base temperature that is calculated by adding together the ambient (room) temperature, that of the flour, and that of the water. Knowing and respecting this principle produces bread of consistent quality. For the

recipes in this book, the base temperature is 129.2-132.8°F (54-56°C) for white bread and 136.4-149°F (58-65°C) for dark bread. Obviously you also need to take into account the temperature of your kitchen, and will readily understand that a difference of 50°F (10°C) can have a significant impact. To simplify the task, water temperature is indicated in the recipes. Before you start kneading, quickly check these three temperatures (flour, water, ambient) to see if you have achieved the average.

KNEADING BY HAND

Make a deep well in the flour and mix in the water, liquid sourdough starter or yeast, and the salt until they begin to be absorbed. This initial process is called "mixing." Kneading properly consists of mixing and then pulling the dough with your fingers, pushing it down, reshaping it, pulling it again, and aerating it to incorporate oxygen—all over a period of 10 minutes or so. As you knead, the structure of the dough will change, becoming smoother and stronger. The proteinaceous network—the gluten strands—begins to develop, creating carbon dioxide (CO_2), which will seek ways of escaping (see also Fermentation, page 24). If the recipe calls for other ingredients (nuts, olives, dried fruits, and so on), these are added at the end of the kneading process.

THE ENERGY OF THE HAND

I strongly believe that energy is transmitted through the hands during the kneading process. All comparative studies I have made throughout my baking life convince me that dough works better if mixed by hand rather than by a machine. I would dearly like to offer our customers hand-kneaded bread, but hygiene laws increasingly tend to remove hands from the baking process. Some readers prefer to start the kneading process in a machine, and then finish it by hand.

KNEADING BY HAND (WET DOUGH)

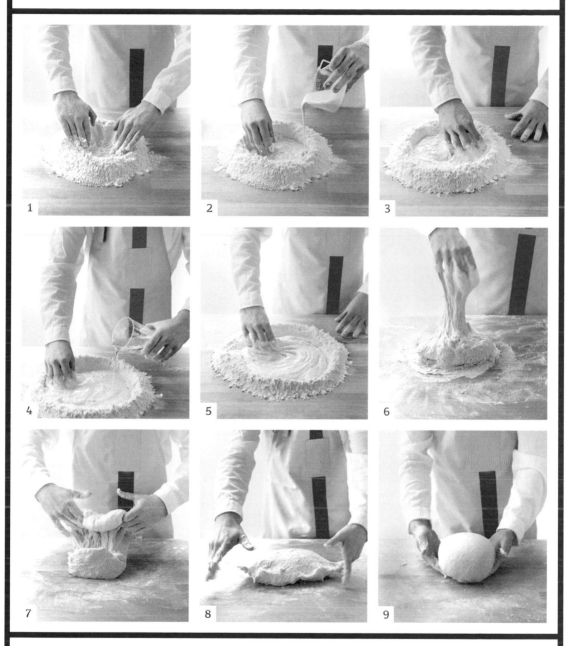

Place the flour on the work surface and make a large well in the center [1]. Add some water, the liquid sourdough starter [2], crumbled yeast, and salt. Mix with one hand [3], while using the other hand to bring the flour gradually in towards the center of the well. As you mix in the flour, the well will start to grow larger and the mixture inside will take on the consistency of thick cream. Add the rest of the water [4] and continue to mix, bringing in the flour gradually until it is fully incorporated [5, 6]. Take hold of the dough with both hands. It will stick to the work surface. Lift it up from the work surface, stretching it gently [7], and then fold it over forcefully to trap air [8]. Repeat several times until the dough becomes smooth and elastic and no longer sticks to the work surface. Roll it over on itself to form a smooth ball [9].

The Basics of Bread Making

KNEADING BY HAND (DRY DOUGH)

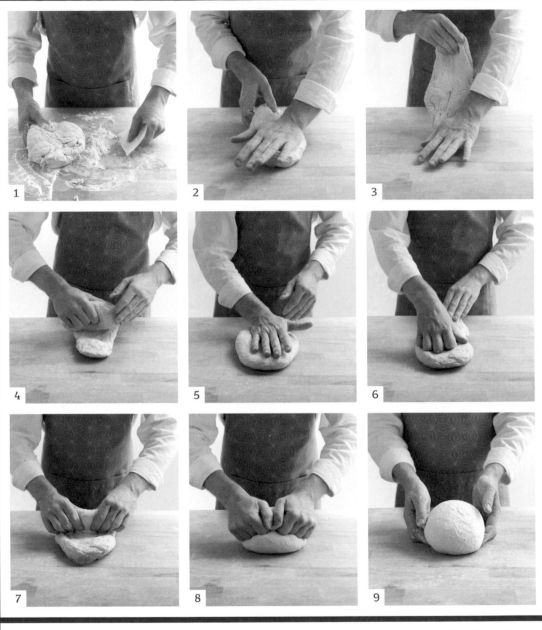

For some kinds of bread, the dough can be fairly firm from the mixing stage. This depends on the quantity of water and also on the type and quality of the flour.

Clear any scraps from the work surface with a dough cutter [1] and roughly shape the dough. Hold it firmly with one hand [2] while pulling and stretching it up with the other hand [3]. Fold it over once or twice [4], then flatten it (also known as "knocking it down") [5]. Repeat the pulling [6] and folding until the dough becomes smooth and elastic, then fold it over on itself [7, 8] and form into a smooth ball [9].

KNEADING IN A STAND MIXER

Place the ingredients in the mixer bowl in the following order: flour, water, liquid sourdough starter, yeast, and salt. The salt should not come into direct contact with the yeast or the starter (if you prefer, dissolve it in the water first). Start the motor at a low speed, to mix the ingredients together. Once they are blended evenly, increase the speed and start the proper kneading process without stopping.

A white, well-aerated crumb requires intensive kneading to aerate the dough. A slow fermentation, on the other hand, requires a slow, short kneading process. As I work with CRC flours, I tend not to knead very much in order to preserve the carotenoid pigments that are essential to the flavor and color of the crumb. It's better to knead a little, and then leave the dough to ferment for a long time, and work with minimal or no additional baker's yeast. It is said that it takes 12 hours to make good bread. For flavorless bread, three hours is enough.

FERMENTATION

Central to the bread-making process, fermentation arises from the development
of natural "wild" yeasts in the dough (the sourdough starter) or from the addition
of commercially developed baker's yeast—or from a combination of the two.
Bakers everywhere manage this process on a daily basis but, in fact, it is a complex
physical-chemical operation. A good understanding of how the mechanisms of
fermentation work will help you bake bread that will delight your family and friends.

WHAT MAKES BREAD RISE?

At the end of the kneading process,
the dough is left to rise on the work surface
or in a bowl, covered with a damp cloth. This
first stage of fermentation is called "rising,"
or in French, *le pointage* (see also page 30).

At this stage the micro-organisms
contained in the flour and the wild yeasts
(as distinct from baker's yeast) begin
to multiply, using other ingredients present
(essentially sugars such as glucose and
maltose), as food. By breaking down these
sugars in an oxygen-deprived (anaerobic)
environment, the micro-organisms convert
carbon dioxide and alcohol (ethanol).
The carbon dioxide gas is what makes the
dough inflate and therefore "rise." The dough's
ability to retain this gas is due to the
formation of wheat proteins (gluten)
in a continuous elastic network during the
kneading process.

FERMENTATION WITH A SOURDOUGH STARTER

Making bread with a natural starter involves
maintaining a balance between the actions
of bacteria and yeasts. The difficulty lies
in the fact that the bacteria (called "lactic,"
because they produce lactic acid) act at
a temperature of around 86°F (30°C) while
the yeasts act best at temperatures between
71.5-78.8°F (22-26°C). Low temperatures
will cause the sourdough bread to
taste overly sour. Kneading, hydration,
temperature, time, and ingredients all affect
the fermentation process.

LIQUID STARTER AND FIRM STARTER

The terms liquid starter and firm starter
are used, depending on the proportions
of water and flour. A liquid starter is
prepared by mixing 50 g (scant ¼ cup)
water with 50 g (scant ½ cup) flour, while
30 g (2 tablespoons) water is sufficient for
a firm starter.

△ All the recipes in this book are made with a
liquid sourdough starter because it is simple to
use: it mixes into the flour as easily as water.
Bear in mind that liquid leaven will represent
between 20-50% of the weight of the flour.

CARING FOR THE STARTER

The starter will remain alive for an average
of 3 days after it has been refreshed.
Accordingly, it should be refreshed at 3-day
intervals by adding 50% of its own weight
in water and flour. For instance, if you
have 300 g of starter remaining, add 75 g
(scant ⅔ cup) flour and 75 g (⅓ cup) water.
Remember that the starter is a living thing
and that you need to nourish it to keep it
alive. If you will not be baking bread for
several days, or if the ambient temperature
rises, seal the jar tightly and store it in the
refrigerator, where it will keep for several
weeks. You can adapt the initial quantity
of starter, depending on how often you plan
to bake.

LIQUID SOURDOUGH STARTER

To make about 500 g (4 cups) liquid sourdough starter

INGREDIENTS

- 140 g (scant 1½ cup) organic light, medium, or dark rye flour
- 240 g (1 cup) water at 86°F (30°C) temperature
- 10 g clear honey (or malt)
- 100 g (generous ¾ cup) all-purpose (plain) flour

DAY 1

Use a spatula to mix 20 g (¼ cup) rye flour with 20 g (4 teaspoons) water in a bowl, then add 5 g (¾ teaspoon) clear honey [1, 2]. Cover with a clean cloth and leave for 24 hours in a warm place. If the starter curdles, begin again.

DAY 2

Bubbles will have formed on the surface. In a larger container mix together 40 g (scant ½ cup) rye flour, 40 g (2⅔ tablespoons) water, and 5 g (¾ teaspoon) clear honey. Stir in the mix from the first day. This is called "feeding" or "refreshing" the starter. Cover with a cloth and leave to ferment for 24 hours.

DAY 3

The mixture will be bubbling noticeably. Mix 80 g (¾ cup) rye flour and 80 g (generous ⅔ cup) water in a larger bowl. Blend in the mix from the second day. Cover with a cloth and leave to ferment for 24 hours [3].

DAY 4

To the third day's mix, add the all-purpose (plain) flour and 100 g (scant ½ cup) water. Stir well. Your starter is now ready to use. It will have the consistency of thick pancake batter. Store it in a glass jar, lightly covered, but so that air can get to the starter. (If you plan to keep it for some time, it should be stored airtight in the refrigerator.)

1

2

3

PRE-FERMENTATION METHODS

Naturally leavened breads may use different methods of pre-fermentation. The dough is kick-started by adding bacteria and complementary yeasts. However, there are various other methods of launching the fermentation process, which can make it possible to reduce the length of the first rise (*le pointage*). Some commercial bakeries use these methods to manage timings better and, most importantly, to improve the taste of the bread.

THE POOLISH METHOD

In a stand mixer or mixing bowl, combine 500 g (4 cups) all-purpose (plain) flour with 500 g (generous 2 cups) water and 3-4 g (1⅓ teaspoons) fresh baker's yeast. Never add salt at this stage, as it will affect the fermentation. Cover the bowl and place in the refrigerator for around 10 hours. Add 20-50% of this preparation to every 500 g (4 cups) flour when mixing.

YEAST PRE-FERMENT

Take one quarter of the flour outlined in the recipe and add 60% of its weight in water (60 g [¼ cup] water to 100 g [generous ¾ cup] flour). Add 1% baker's yeast (10 g [3 teaspoons] per kg of flour) and mix well. Place in the refrigerator for 6-10 hours. Add 20-50% of the yeast pre-ferment to every 500 g (4 cups) flour when mixing.

AUTOLYSE

This pre-fermentation method is really a mixing process. Mix the flour and water together for 4 minutes on slow speed if using a stand mixer, or 5 minutes by hand— it's simply a question of blending them thoroughly. Leave the dough to rest for an hour, or up to 10 hours if you want to improve the flavor of the bread. Then add the other ingredients and knead. This technique helps the gluten develop more quickly, gives a more elastic dough, and reduces the length of kneading time.

FERMENTED DOUGH

This is dough with added yeast, which is prepared the night before and left overnight in the refrigerator. When you are ready to make the bread, the fermented dough is added to the flour in the proportion of 15-30% of the weight of the flour. For instance, to 500 g (4 cups) flour, add 75-150 g fermented dough just before kneading.

HOW TO MAKE A STARTER WITH APPLES OR GRAPES
Take 500 g (17½ oz) organic apples or grapes. Wash and slice them, leaving the skin on. Place in a bowl, cover with a cloth, and leave to ferment at ambient temperature for 10-15 days. Strain and collect the juice that the fruit releases. Mix 200 ml (scant 1 cup) of this juice with 400 g (3 cups) rye flour, and let rest for 24 hours. The next day, add 100 g (generous ¾ cup) flour and 100 g (scant ½ cup) water. Repeat on the following day. You now have enough yeasts to impregnate the dough.

The Basics of Bread Making

FRESH YEAST IN BREAD MAKING

While yeast was long used for fermenting beer, its use in baking varied wildly up until the nineteenth century. It was Louis Pasteur who demonstrated that yeast fermentation was caused by the growth of anaerobic micro-organisms that can live without oxygen. A number of cultures were subsequently isolated, notably *Saccharomyces cerevisiae*, which we call baker's yeast.

When making bread with yeast, the "wild" micro-flora naturally present in the flour do not have time to activate because of the large quantity of *S. cerevisiae* which is introduced into the mixture (1 g represents between 9–10 billion cells). This speeds up the alcoholic fermentation process. It produces a quantity of carbon dioxide that encourages the formation of air bubbles in the bread, of ethanol that evaporates during cooking, and of various chemicals that add different aromas.

YEAST AS AN AID TO NATURAL STARTERS

If used in the correct proportion, yeast need not be avoided entirely. Some breads made through yeast fermentation can taste pretty good. I add a small quantity to most of my sourdough recipes. Yeast can be used if you need to fine-tune the fermentation time, but not to sidestep it. If its use is limited to that of supporting role, yeast can prove a marvelous ingredient, as it will correct over-acidic natural starters.

THE HISTORY OF YEAST BREAD
The first yeast manufacturers appeared between 1850-55. The increased availability of commercial yeast encouraged bakers gradually to abandon the traditional, more demanding leaven method of making bread. They began by simply adding yeast to the starter to give a less dense, more aerated bread. After World War II, the French understandably wanted to forget dense, indigestible black bread, and bakers seized the opportunity to offer a substantial, quick-rising bread (that required no advance preparation) to their customers. Consumers took to it, and there was no turning back. Bakers gradually increased their yeast content in order to reduce fermentation time and improve productivity. They added more salt to corrected poor flavor. Inferior quality flours were not sufficient to feed these sorts of yeasts, so bakers began to use malt-based additives to aid fermentation. These amylases transformed the flour's starch into sugar, while ascorbic acid was added to reinforce the gluten network. By the 1990s, the baking profession began to question these methods.

The Basics of Bread Making

THE TWO STAGES OF FERMENTATION

The fermentation process can be divided into a first rise (*le pointage* in French), which is a "bulk" fermentation before the dough has been portioned, and a second proofing (or *l'apprêt* in French), after the dough has been portioned and shaped.

FIRST RISE

After kneading, the dough is left at room temperature in a draft-free area to rest and relax, covered with a slightly damp cloth to prevent a crust forming. As it ferments, carbon dioxide is released, which causes the dough to increase in size. As it rises, the gluten strands, created by kneading, stretch and give the dough structure. The dough will double in size, depending on the ambient temperature and the type of starter. This transformation is accompanied by acidification (see below).

This first fermentation can last between 1-3 hours (more in some cases), depending on the flours used and the ambient temperature. There is no need to prolong it if you have used any of the pre-fermentation methods on page 26 (poolish, yeast pre-ferment, autolyse, or fermented dough). My advice is to use a mixture of knowledge and instinct. It is important to keep an eye on the dough as it rises, but it is also essential to understand the forces that come into play during the fermentation so that you know how to manage them. If you give a dough that ferments at 64.5°F (18°C) the same fermentation time as a 75°F (24°C) dough, when you should have doubled or even tripled it, you are not giving your bread the best chance to achieve its full flavor potential. It's a good idea to equip yourself with a digital probe thermometer (available from specialist stores).

PROOFING

This second fermentation comes after the dough is shaped and just before baking. As with the first rise, the dough is covered with a damp cloth and left at room temperature in a draft-free area. To achieve a well-aerated crumb during baking it is important to preserve the carbon dioxide that develops inside the bread. When sliced, any irregular air bubbles in the crumb will show how well the fermentation process has been managed.

△ WARM BREAD FOR BREAKFAST
In a bakery, the shaped loaves are placed in a rising chamber at a controlled temperature that is geared to the time of baking. This means the bakery can offer customers freshly baked bread at any time of day. For hot bread at breakfast, you can reproduce this method at home. How is this done? The day before, after the first rise, shape the loaves at around 5 p.m., place them in a tightly sealed container, and refrigerate. At such a low temperature (around 39°F [4°C]) the dough will not rise much and will keep well for 10-12 hours. The next morning, all you have to do is pop the dough in the oven to bake.

ACIDITY OF THE DOUGH

The pH scale is used to measure the acidity in a dough, as an aid to evaluating the fermentation process (the more acidic the bread, the lower the pH number). At the beginning of the first fermentation the pH is around 6-7 (depending on the kneading and the starter used). By the end of fermentation a typical bread will have a pH of 5-6. Current regulation fixes the pH of sourdough bread at 4-4.3.

A pH between 4-5 delivers rich aroma compounds (specialists have identified around 200) and a good "keeping" quality. Pharmacies stock pH kits (acid-alkaline indicators) that help to measure pH levels.

The Basics of Bread Making

PRE-SHAPING

After the first rise, the dough is divided into portions with a dough cutter. These portions are then weighed to make sure they are of the desired weight. Next comes the preliminary shaping of the dough, which should be done briskly, so as to work the dough as little as possible.

At this stage, the shape of the dough is determined by the final appearance of the loaf of bread. So for round or oval loaves, the dough should first be roughly shaped into round balls. Long breads, such as baguettes, *ficelles* or *epis*, are shaped into a rectangle: the portions of dough are simply rolled over themselves and very slightly stretched. After this first shaping, the dough is left to rest or "relax" for a fairly short period before the final shaping.

PRE-SHAPING INTO A ROUND BALL
1

Fold the dough over on itself [1] on a non-floured work surface. When the seam is underneath [2], roll over and down until it forms a well-rounded ball [3].

PRE-SHAPING INTO A ROUND BALL 2

If the lump of dough is small, use your hands to roll it on a non-floured work surface [1, 2] until it forms a well-rounded ball [3].

PRE-SHAPING INTO A RECTANGLE

Flatten the lump of dough [1]. Roll it over itself [2, 3] on a non-floured work surface.

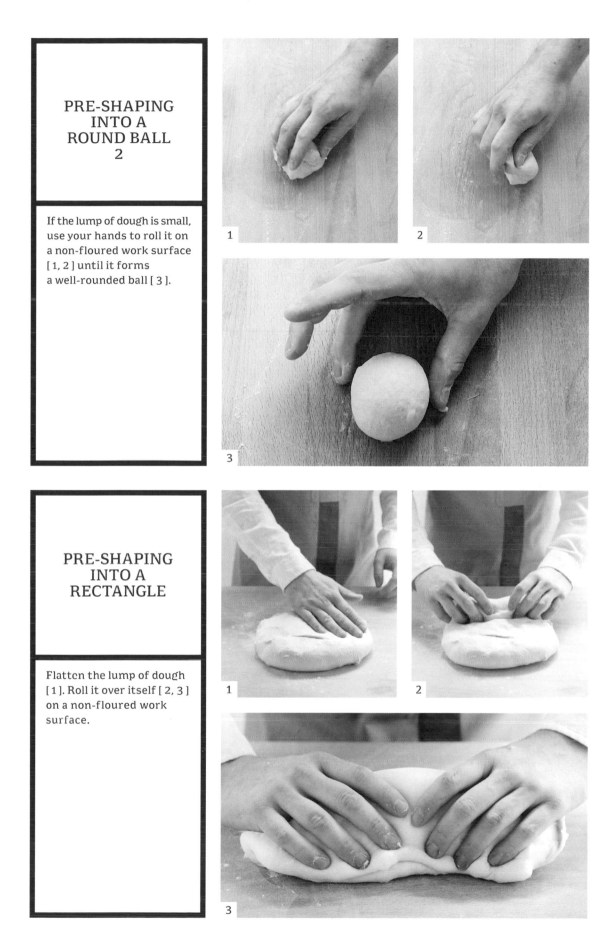

FINAL SHAPING

This process has a direct influence on the final appearance of the loaf. French bread comes in many shapes; here are the suggested methods for shaping three of the most popular.

FREEZING THE DOUGH
You can freeze freshly shaped pieces of dough. When you're ready to bake, allow them to defrost at room temperature and undergo a second fermentation before scoring and putting them in the oven.

SHAPING A ROUND LOAF
1

On a lightly floured work surface, carefully flatten the dough with the palm of your hand [1]. Fold the edges in towards the center [2] and press down on the seam without using too much force. Roll the dough over on itself until the seam is underneath. Shape it between your hands while pressing down on the work surface [3] to create a well-rounded ball [4].

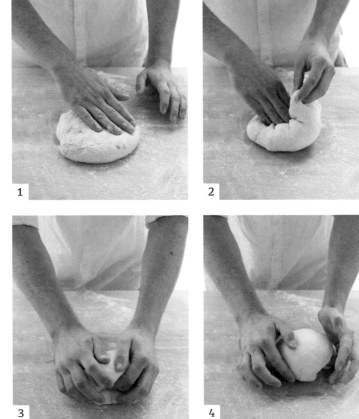

1

2

3

4

SHAPING A ROUND LOAF 2

In some cases, a ball of dough is not flattened [1], but is just turned between the hands while pressing down on the work surface [2] to create a well-rounded ball [3].

1

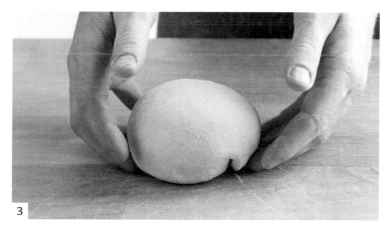

2

3

SHAPING A BATARD

On a floured work surface, flatten the dough with the palm of your hand. Fold it over twice and press down with your fingers [1]. Swivel the dough 180 degrees [2], fold in again lengthwise by a third and press down along the edge [3]. Fold the dough in half lengthwise and seal the edges together by pressing with the heel of the hand [4]. Roll with lightly floured hands to the desired length [5, 6].

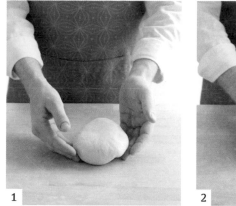

1

2

3

4

5

6

The Basics of Bread Making

SHAPING
A BAGUETTE

On a lightly floured work surface, carefully flatten the dough with the palm of your hand [1]. With the long side facing you, fold in a third towards the center and press along the edge with the heel of your hand [2] or with your fingertips. Swivel the dough 180 degrees [3]. Fold in the other long edge so that it overlaps in the center and press down again [4]. Fold this side up and on top of the other [5] and seal the edges together with the heel of your hand [6, 7]. Roll with lightly floured hands to the desired length [8] and pinch the ends into a point.

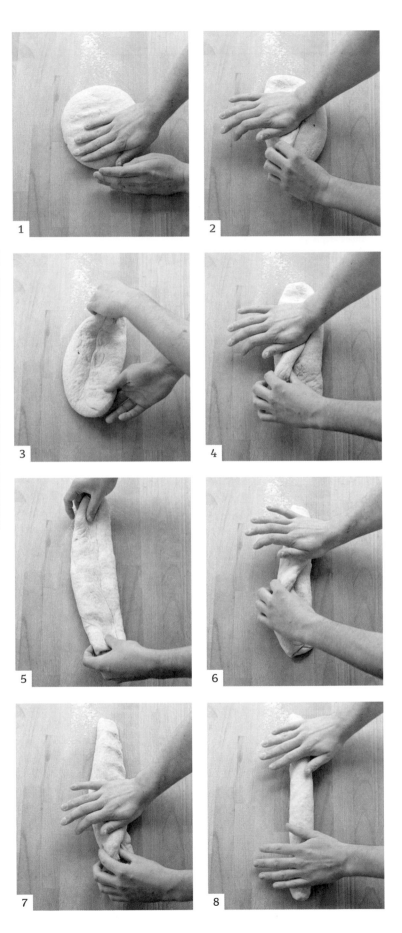

The Basics of Bread Making

SCORING THE DOUGH

During the baking, the carbon dioxide that has been created during fermentation, and which is held in place by the network of gluten strands, turns into steam and will try to escape. To control the direction in which the dough expands, it is important to manage the "openings" in the last stage of proofing. This is done by scoring, or finely slashing, the dough.

SCORING, SLASHING, NICKING, INCISING

These various expressions all refer to the technique of cutting into the dough to create a sort of chimney in the baking bread. The dough is usually scored with a sharp blade (a dough cutter or special razor-sharp baker's "lame") mounted on a handle. The depth of the incisions depends on the level of the fermentation: the more the dough has risen, the shallower the cuts. Scoring is usually done just before the bread is due to go into the oven.

Illustrated below are 10 common ways of scoring dough:
- Cross shape
- Square
- Polka or crosshatch
- Pithivier or swirl
- Single slash
- Double slash
- Four slashes
- Sausage cut
- Chevron
- Hedgehog cut

CROSS SHAPE

SQUARE

POLKA OR CROSSHATCH

PITHIVIER OR SWIRL

SINGLE SLASH

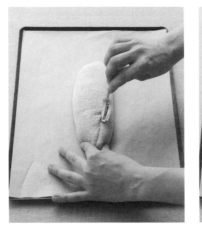

DOUBLE SLASH

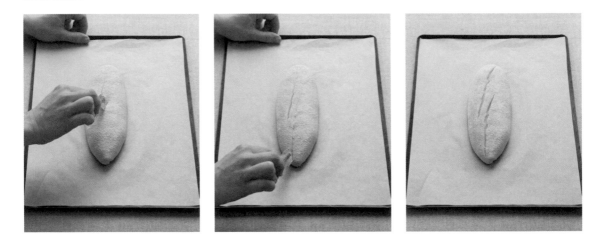

FOUR SLASHES

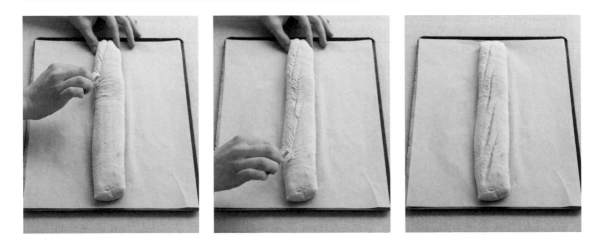

SAUSAGE CUT

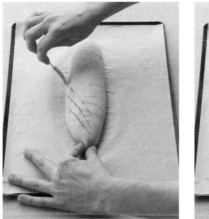

CHEVRON

HEDGEHOG CUT

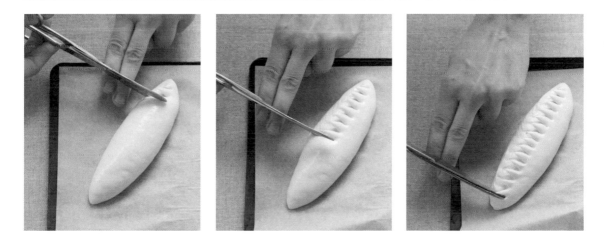

The Basics of Bread Making

BAKING & STORING BREAD

With a bit of planning, it is perfectly possible to bake bread successfully in a home oven. All the breads in this book have been tested in this kind of oven, and the differences between them and bread produced in a commercial bakery are often tiny: crust thickness, color, finish of the scoring. These are all barely noticeable differences and none should discourage you from baking bread in your own home!

THE OVEN

You will get the best results with a convection oven, especially for breads that require a long baking time. The most important thing is to preheat the oven to the instructed temperature; otherwise, the scoring will not develop. (French bakers speak of scoring that does not "throw" or "spit.")

SIMULTANEOUS BAKING ON TWO SHELVES

When you have to prepare several loaves, they can be baked simultaneously on two shelves. In a traditional oven—not a fan-assisted one—it may be necessary to switch the shelves around halfway through the process to ensure even baking.

STONE-BAKED BREAD

This is done with a "baking stone," also known as a "pizza stone." The stone should be placed on a rack in the lower shelf of the oven and preheated for an hour. It will retain the heat and transfer it to the bread directly during baking. Use a small wooden paddle, or baker's peel, to slide the dough on and off the stone.

A TOUCH OF STEAM

Bread should be baked in a steam-filled oven. The steam slows the drying of the dough but encourages the development of a good, well-colored crust and a moist, well-flavored crumb. The best way to create steam is to preheat a baking pan in the bottom of the oven and add 50 g (scant ¼ cup) of water just before putting the bread in to bake. Failing that, you could also brush or spray the dough lightly.

COOLING

When the bread is baked, take it out of the oven and leave it to cool on a wire rack. This is known as "sweating": excess moisture continues to evaporate and the bread will reduce in weight by up to 2%.

STORING BREAD

Long loaves with a highly aerated crumb and a fine crust will lose their freshness and become stale more rapidly than large round loaves with a dense, compact crumb. In general, natural—or sourdough—fermentation ensures that a loaf of bread can be kept for several days without going stale. By contrast, a well-baked baguette will only keep for 8–10 hours. It's best to wrap bread in paper, linen, or cotton bags, rather than in plastic, which will make it sweat. Store in a dry place rather than in the refrigerator, where it will go stale more quickly.

The Basics of Bread Making

LEARNING FROM MISTAKES

You may experience a few setbacks when you embark on the great bread-making adventure. Remember that it is less a question of following recipes than of listening to your instincts and observing how the dough evolves. The potential for error will be different every time you bake, since the dough itself is never exactly the same.

It's up to you to analyze each challenge that arises. However, you should always view mistakes positively: each one gives you a better understanding of what happens at the different stages of baking, and so helps your progress. To help you along, here are a few of the problems you might encounter at different stages of baking, along with their likely causes.

The scoring doesn't "catch." The split in the lower left-hand side of the loaf shows that the carbon dioxide wasn't able to escape through the scoring on the loaf.

The brioche in the lower pan has been proofed for too long and collapsed as soon as it was scored.

THE DOUGH IS TOO WET
- There was too much water in the dough
- The water was too hot
- The kneading was insufficient

THE LOAVES ARE RATHER FLAT
- There was a problem with the flour
- The starter was not sufficiently "active"
- The dough was too cold
- The dough was either too stiff or too soft
- The dough was proofed for too long
- The oven temperature was too low or too high

THE LOAVES LACK VOLUME
- The flour was too "strong"
- The starter was not sufficiently "active"
- The dough was too cold
- The dough was proofed for too long
- The dough was over-worked (with too much force)

THE DOUGH DEVELOPED A CRUST
- The scoring was inadequate
- The oven temperature was too low or too high
- There wasn't enough steam when putting the dough in the oven

THE BREAD HAS A DENSE, UNAERATED CRUMB
- The first rise or proofing was insufficient
- The dough was over-worked during the shaping (was too firm)
- The scoring was inadequate
- The oven temperature was too high
- There wasn't enough steam when putting the dough in the oven

THE BAGUETTES ARE CURVED OR BENT
- The dough was over-kneaded (was too firm)
- The dough was over-worked during the shaping (was too firm; too tight)
- The oven temperature was too high

THE SCORINGS DO NOT "CATCH" (THEY DISAPPEAR DURING BAKING)
- The kneading was insufficient
- The dough was over-worked (with too much force)
- The dough wasn't properly shaped
- The dough was over-proofed
- The scoring was too shallow
- The oven temperature was too high
- There was too much steam when putting the dough in the oven

THE CRUST IS TOO PALE
- The flour was poor quality
- The dough was over-proved
- The dough was worked too much during the kneading and/or shaping
- The oven temperature too low
- The bread wasn't baked for long enough
- There wasn't enough steam when putting the dough in the oven

THE CRUST IS DULL
- There wasn't enough salt
- The dough was over-worked
- The dough was too warm
- There wasn't enough steam when putting the dough in the oven

THE CRUST IS SOFT
- The dough was too cold
- The dough wasn't properly shaped
- There was too much steam when putting the dough in the oven
- The bread was undercooked
- The bread wasn't cooled properly

THE BASE OF THE BREAD IS SOMEWHAT BURNT
- The oven temperature was too high
- The baking sheet was placed too low in the oven

The Basics of Bread Making

TRADITIONAL
LOAVES

BOULE

Makes 1 boule, about 920 g

TIMINGS
- Mixing & kneading: 10 min
- First rising: 1h 30 min
- Proofing: 2h
- Baking: 40–45 min

INGREDIENTS
- 500 g (4 cups) all-purpose (plain) flour
- 350 g (1 1/2 cups) water at 68°F (20°C)
- 100 g (scant 1/2 cup) liquid sourdough starter (or 25 g [3 tablespoons] dry sourdough starter)
- 2 g (1/2 teaspoon) fresh baker's yeast, crumbled
- 10 g (2 teaspoons) salt

KNEADING IN A STAND MIXER

Put all the ingredients in the bowl. Knead with the dough hook for 4 minutes at low speed, then 6 minutes at high speed.

KNEADING BY HAND

Put the flour on a work surface or in a mixing bowl and make a large well in the center. Pour in half the water, then add the starter, fresh yeast, and salt. Mix well, then add the remaining water and blend until all the flour is incorporated. Knead the dough until it becomes smooth and elastic [1].

Shape the dough into a ball and cover with a damp cloth. Let rise for 1 hour 30 minutes to 2 hours. It will have increased in volume by the end of the rising time [2].

Place the dough on a lightly floured work surface. Turn it over, then bring the edges in towards the center [3] and press them down gently. Turn the dough over again and shape it between your hands, while pressing down on the work surface, to create a well-rounded ball [4]. Cover with a damp cloth and leave to proof for 2 hours.

Place a baking sheet on the bottom shelf of the oven and preheat to 450°F (230°C). Transfer the dough onto another baking sheet lined with parchment (baking) paper. Score the surface in a crosshatch pattern (see page 39). Just before putting it in the oven, pour 50 g (scant 1/4 cup) of water onto the preheated baking sheet. Bake for 40–45 minutes.

Remove from the oven and leave to cool on a wire rack.

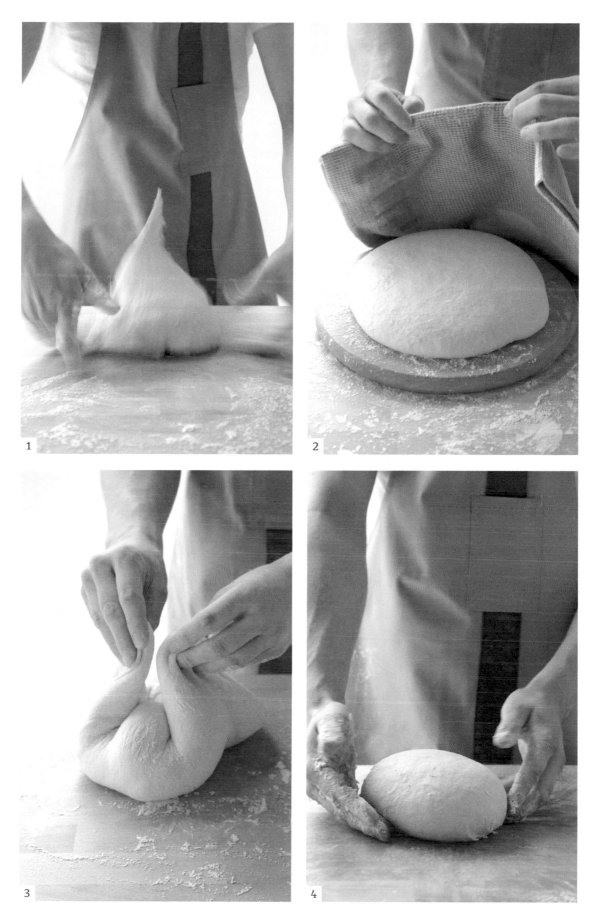

Traditional Breads

Boule

BATARD

Makes 3 batards,
each about 300 g

TIMINGS

- Mixing & kneading: 10 min
- First rising: 1h 30 min
- Resting: 30 min
- Proofing: 1h 30 min
- Baking: 20 min

INGREDIENTS

- 500 g (4 cups) all-purpose (plain) flour, plus extra for dusting
- 330 g (1⅓ cups) water at 68°F (20°C)
- 100 g (scant ½ cup) liquid sourdough starter (or 25 g [3 tablespoons] dry sourdough starter)
- 3 g (1 teaspoon) fresh baker's yeast, crumbled
- 10 g (2 teaspoons) salt

KNEADING IN A STAND MIXER

Put all the ingredients in the bowl. Knead with the dough hook for 4 minutes at slow speed, then for 6 minutes at high speed.

KNEADING BY HAND

Put the flour on a work surface or in a mixing bowl and make a large well in the center. Add half the water, then add the starter, fresh yeast, and salt. Mix well, then add the remaining water and blend until all the flour is incorporated. Knead the dough until it becomes smooth and elastic.

Shape the dough into a ball and cover with a damp cloth. Leave to rise for 1 hour 30 minutes. It will have increased in volume by the end of the rising time.

Dust the work surface. Divide the dough into 3 equal pieces and shape them into balls. Cover with a damp cloth and leave to rest for 30 minutes.

Working with 1 piece of dough at a time, use the palm of your hand to flatten it gently into a rough oval. With the long side facing you, fold in a third towards the center and press along the edge with your fingertips. Swivel the dough 180 degrees. Fold in the other long edge so that it overlaps in the center and press with your fingertips. Fold one half on top of the other, and seal the edges together with the heel of your hand. With lightly floured hands, roll the dough out to form a plump oval, slightly tapered at each end. Shape the other 2 loaves the same way.

Place the loaves, seams underneath, on a baking sheet lined with parchment (baking) paper. Cover with a damp cloth and leave to proof for 1 hour 30 minutes.

Place another baking sheet on the bottom shelf of the oven and preheat to 450°F (230°C). Score each loaf once, lengthwise. Just before putting the loaves in the oven, pour 50 g (scant ¼ cup) of water onto the preheated baking sheet. Bake for 20 minutes.

Remove from the oven and leave to cool on a wire rack.

BAGUETTE

Makes 3 baguettes,
each about 300 g

TIMINGS
- Mixing & kneading: 15 min
- First resting: 1 h
- First rising: 1 h 30 min
- Second resting: 30 min
- Proofing: 1 h 40 min
- Baking: 20 min

INGREDIENTS
- 500 g (4 cups) all-purpose (plain) flour, plus extra for dusting
- 325 g (scant 1⅓ cups) water at 68°F (20°C)
- 100 g (scant ½ cup) liquid sourdough starter (or 25 g [3 tablespoons] dry sourdough starter)
- 3 g (1 teaspoon) fresh baker's yeast, crumbled
- 10 g (2 teaspoons) salt

KNEADING IN A STAND MIXER
Put the flour and water in the bowl and mix for 4 minutes at low speed. Remove the bowl from the machine and cover it with a damp cloth. Leave to rest for 1 hour, then add the starter, fresh yeast, and salt. Knead with the dough hook for 4 minutes at low speed, then for 7 minutes at high speed.

KNEADING BY HAND
Put the flour on a work surface or in a mixing bowl and make a large well in the center. Pour in two-thirds of the water and mix until all the flour has been incorporated. Leave to rest for 1 hour under a damp cloth, then incorporate the rest of the water, the starter, fresh yeast, and salt. Knead the dough until it becomes smooth and elastic.

Shape into a ball and cover with a damp cloth. Let rise for 1 hour 30 minutes. It will have increased in volume by the end of the rising time.

Dust the work surface. Divide the dough into 3 equal pieces. Fold each piece over on itself, pulling gently to stretch into a longish log. Cover with a damp cloth and leave to rest for 30 minutes.

Working with 1 piece of dough at a time, use the palm of your hand to flatten it gently. With the long side facing you, fold in a third towards the center and press along the edge with your fingertips [1]. Swivel the dough 180 degrees. Fold in the other long edge so that it overlaps in the center and press with the heel of your hand. Fold one half on top of the other, and seal the edges together with the heel of your hand [2].

With lightly floured hands, roll the baguette out to 21 inches (55 cm) long, then pinch each end into a point [3]. Shape the other 2 baguettes the same way.

Carefully lift the baguettes onto a lightly floured baker's cloth, seams underneath. Separate them by making folds in the cloth. Cover with a damp cloth and leave to proof for 1 hour 40 minutes, by which time the baguettes will have increased in volume [4].

Place a baking sheet on the bottom shelf of the oven and preheat to 450°F (230°C). Gently place the baguettes, seam down, on another baking sheet lined with parchment (baking) paper. Dust with flour and make 4 evenly spaced oblique slashes along the length of each baguette [5]. Just before putting the baguettes in the oven, pour 50 g (scant ¼ cup) of water onto the preheated baking sheet. Bake for 20 minutes.

Remove from the oven and leave to cool on a wire rack.

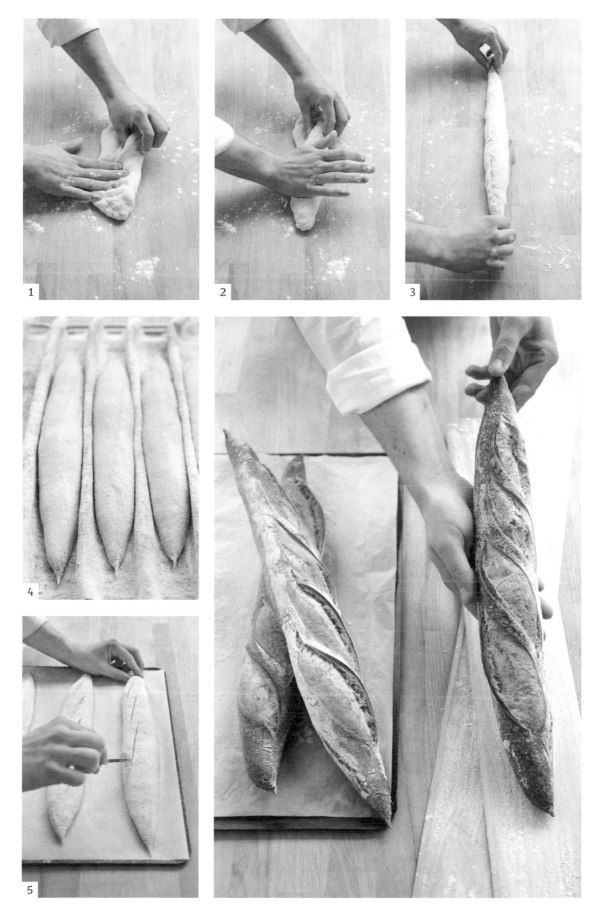

Traditional Breads

POLKA
BREAD

Makes 2 loaves, each
about 460 g

TIMINGS
- Mixing & kneading: 16 min
- First resting: 1h
- First rising: 1h 30 min
- Second resting: 30 min
- Proofing: 1h 30 min
- Baking: 25 min

INGREDIENTS
- 500 g (4 cups) all-purpose
  (plain) flour
- 325 g (scant 1⅓ cups)
  water at 68°F (20°C)
- 100 g (scant ½ cup)
  liquid sourdough starter
  (or 25 g [3 tablespoons]
  dry sourdough starter)
- 3 g (1 teaspoon) fresh
  baker's yeast, crumbled
- 10 g (2 teaspoons) salt

KNEADING IN A STAND MIXER

Put the flour and water in the bowl. Knead with the dough hook for 5 minutes at slow speed. Remove the bowl from the mixer and cover with a damp cloth. Leave to rest for 1 hour. Add the starter, the fresh yeast, and the salt. Knead for 4 minutes at slow speed, then for 7 minutes at high speed.

KNEADING BY HAND

Put the flour on a work surface or in a mixing bowl and make a large well in the center. Pour in two-thirds of the water and mix until all the flour is incorporated. Leave to rest for 1 hour under a damp cloth, then incorporate the remaining water, the starter, fresh yeast, and salt. Knead the dough until it becomes smooth and elastic.

Shape the dough into a ball and cover with a damp cloth. Leave to rise for 1 hour 30 minutes. It will have increased in volume by the end of the rising time.

Dust the work surface. Divide the dough in 2 equal pieces. Fold each piece over on itself, pulling gently to stretch into a longish log. Cover with a damp cloth and leave to rest for 30 minutes.

Working with 1 piece of dough at a time, use the palm of your hand to flatten it gently [1]. With the long side facing you, fold in a third towards the center and press it gently with the heel of your hand [2]. Swivel the dough 180 degrees. Fold in the other long edge so that it overlaps in the center and press again. Fold one half on top of the other, and seal the edges together with the heel of your hand. With lightly floured hands, roll the loaf out to around 20 inches (50 cm), tapering the ends. Repeat with the other loaf.

Place the polkas on a baking sheet lined with parchment (baking) paper, seams underneath. Dust with flour [3], then use a light board to flatten them [4]. Cover with a damp cloth and leave to proof for 1 hour 30 minutes.

Place another baking sheet on the bottom shelf of the oven and preheat to 450°F (230°C). Score the loaves in a crosshatch pattern (see page 39) [5]. Just before putting the loaves in the oven, pour 50 g (scant ¼ cup) of water onto the preheated baking sheet. Bake for 25 minutes.

Remove from the oven and leave to cool on a wire rack.

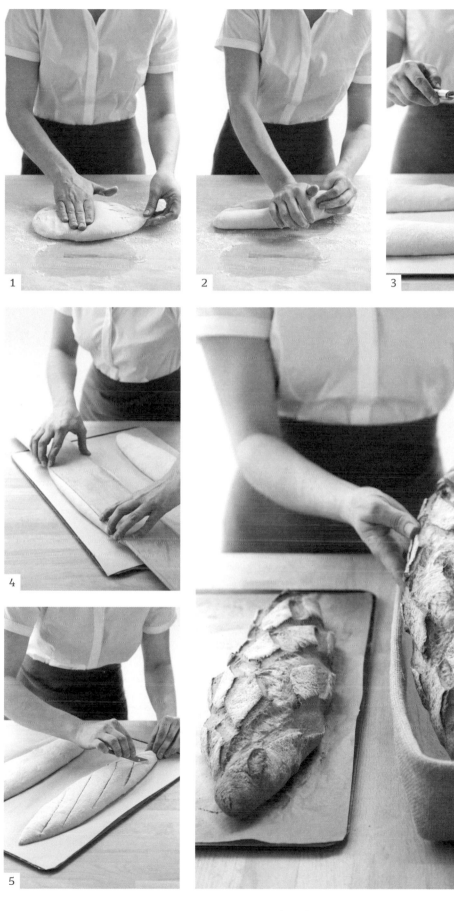

Traditional Breads

FANCY LOAVES: FICELLE, EPI, & BRAIDED

Makes 3 ficelles and 3 epi, each about 155 g, or 3 braids, each about 310 g

TIMINGS
- Mixing & kneading: 16 min
- First resting: 1 h
- First rising: 1 h 30 min
- Second resting: 30 min
- Proofing: 1 h 30 min
- Baking: 12–13 or 20 min, depending on the bread

INGREDIENTS
- 500 g (4 cups) all-purpose (plain) flour, plus extra for dusting
- 325 g (scant 1⅓ cups) water at 68°F (20°C)
- 100 g (scant ½ cup) liquid sourdough starter (or 25 g [3 tablespoons] dry sourdough starter)
- 3 g (1 teaspoon) fresh baker's yeast, crumbled
- 10 g (2 teaspoons) salt

KNEADING IN A STAND MIXER

Put the flour and water in the bowl. Knead with the dough hook for 5 minutes at low speed. Remove the bowl from the mixer and cover with a damp cloth. Leave to rest for 1 hour, then add the starter, fresh yeast, and salt. Knead for 4 minutes at low speed, then for 7 minutes at high speed.

KNEADING BY HAND

Put the flour on a work surface or in a mixing bowl and make a large well in the center. Pour in two-thirds of the water and mix until all the flour has been incorporated. Leave to rest for 1 hour, covered with a damp cloth, then incorporate the rest of the water, the starter, baker's yeast, and salt. Knead the dough until it becomes smooth and elastic.

Shape the dough into a ball and cover with a damp cloth. Leave to rise for 1 hour 30 minutes. It will have increased in volume by the end of the rising time.

Dust the work surface. To make 3 ficelles and 3 epis, divide the dough into 6 equal pieces. Fold each piece over on itself, pulling gently to stretch into a longish log. Leave to rest for 30 minutes under a damp cloth.

Working with 1 piece of dough at a time, use the palm of your hand to flatten it gently. With the long side facing you, fold in a third towards the center and press it gently with the heel of your hand. Swivel the dough 180 degrees. Fold in the other long edge so that it overlaps in the center and press again. Fold one half on top of the other, and seal the edges together with the heel of your hand. With lightly floured hands, roll the loaf out to around 20 inches (50 cm), tapering the ends. Shape the other loaves in the same way.

You can now continue on to make either ficelle loaves (see page 59) or epi (see page 60). To make 3 braided loaves, turn to page 62.

FICELLE

Place 3 shaped pieces of dough, seams underneath, on a baking sheet lined with parchment (baking) paper. Cover with a damp cloth and leave to proof for 1 hour 30 minutes.

Place another baking sheet on the bottom shelf of the oven and preheat to 450°F (230°C). Dust the ficelles very lightly with flour [1]. Score 4 or 5 light, oblique incisions along the loaves, beginning each new incision about one-third higher than the preceding one [2, 3].

Just before putting the ficelles in the oven, pour 50 g (scant ¼ cup) of water onto the preheated baking sheet. Bake for 12–13 minutes.

Remove from the oven and leave to cool on a wire rack.

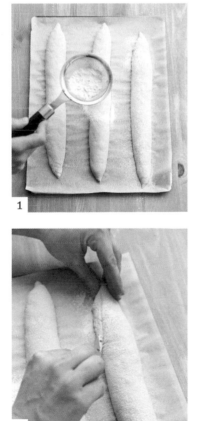

Place 3 shaped pieces of dough, seams underneath, on a baking sheet lined with parchment (baking) paper. Cover with a damp cloth and leave to proof for 1 hour 30 minutes.

Place another baking sheet on the bottom shelf of the oven and preheat to 450°F (230°C).

Flour the blades of a pair of scissors. Using the scissors, held horizontally and at a slight angle, make 5 cuts along the dough at regular intervals, to create 6 "wheat grains" [1]. Use your fingers to gently twist the "grains" alternately to the right and left [2, 3].

Just before putting the loaves in the oven, pour 50 g (scant ¼ cup) of water onto the preheated baking sheet. Bake for around 20 minutes.

Remove from the oven and leave to cool on a wire rack.

After the first rising, divide the dough into 9 equal pieces. Roll them between your hands to make small balls. Cover with a damp cloth and leave to rest for 30 minutes.

Working with 1 piece of dough at a time, use the palm of your hand to flatten it gently into a rough oval. With the long side facing you, fold in a third towards the center and press along the edge with your fingertips. Swivel the dough 180 degrees. Fold in the other long edge so that it overlaps in the center and press with the heel of your hand. Fold one half on top of the other, and seal the edges together with the heel of your hand. With lightly floured hands, roll the dough out to form a strip around 12 inches (30 cm) long and around ⅝ inch (1.5 cm) in diameter, slightly thicker at the center. Repeat with the other 8 pieces of dough.

Take 3 strips and join them together at 1 end. Braid the strips together [1, 2] and firmly seal the ends. Make 2 more braids in the same way. Place the braids on a baking sheet lined with parchment (baking) paper [3]. Cover with a damp cloth and leave to proof for 1 hour 30 minutes.

Place another baking sheet on the bottom shelf of the oven and preheat to 450°F (230°C). Just before putting the braids in the oven, pour 50 g (scant ¼ cup) of water onto the preheated baking sheet. Bake for around 20 minutes. Remove from the oven and leave to cool on a wire rack.

1

2

3

Traditional Breads

BAKER'S PEEL

Makes 3 loaves,
each about 300 g

TIMINGS

- Mixing & kneading: 10 min
- First rising: 1h 30 min
- Resting: 30 min
- Proofing: 1h 30 min
- Baking: 18 min

INGREDIENTS

- 500 g (4 cups) all-purpose (plain) flour, plus extra for dusting
- 350 g (1¼ cups) water at 68°F (20°C)
- 100 g (scant ½ cup) liquid sourdough starter (or 25 g [3 tablespoons] dry sourdough starter)
- 3 g (1 teaspoon) fresh baker's yeast, crumbled
- 10 g (2 teaspoons) salt

In Normandy and Brittany, this bread is known as *une gâche*, which is a type of flat, rounded loaf named after a baker's peel, or paddle.

KNEADING IN A STAND MIXER
Put all the ingredients in the bowl. Knead with the dough hook for 4 minutes at low speed, then for 6 minutes at high speed.

KNEADING BY HAND
Put the flour on the work surface or in a mixing bowl and make a large well in the center. Pour in half the water, then add the starter, fresh yeast, and salt. Mix well, then pour in the rest of the water and blend until all the flour is incorporated. Knead the dough until it is smooth and elastic.

Shape the dough into a ball and cover it with a damp cloth. Leave to rise for 1 hour 30 minutes. By the end of the rising time the dough will have increased in volume.

Dust the work surface. Divide the dough into 3 equal pieces and shape each into a ball. Cover with a damp cloth and leave to rest for 30 minutes.

Carefully flatten the pieces of dough into thick circles, each about 6 inches (15 cm) in diameter. Lift them onto a floured baker's cloth, seams on top, and cover with a damp cloth. Leave to proof for 1 hour 30 minutes.

Place a baking sheet on the bottom shelf of the oven and preheat to 450°F (230°C). Transfer the circles, seams underneath, to another baking sheet lined with parchment (baking) paper. Score a large square on the surface (see page 39). Just before putting the loaves in the oven, pour 50 g (scant ¼ cup) of water onto the preheated baking sheet. Bake for around 18 minutes.

Remove from the oven and leave to cool on a wire rack.

PETITE BAGUETTE

Makes 2 loaves,
each about 460 g

TIMINGS
- Mixing & kneading: 16 min
- First resting: 1h
- First rising: 1h15min
- Second resting: 30 min
- Proofing: 2h
- Baking: 35 min

INGREDIENTS
- 500 g (4 cups) all-purpose (plain) flour, plus extra for dusting
- 330 g (1⅓ cups) water at 68°F (20°C)
- 100 g (scant ½ cup) liquid sourdough starter (or 25 g [3 tablespoons] dry sourdough starter)
- 3 g (1 teaspoon) fresh baker's yeast, crumbled
- 10 g (2 teaspoons) salt

KNEADING IN A STAND MIXER
Put the flour and water in the bowl. Knead with the dough hook for 5 minutes at slow speed. Remove the bowl from the mixer and cover it with a damp cloth. Leave to rest for 1 hour, then add the starter, fresh yeast, and salt. Knead for 4 minutes at slow speed, then 7 minutes at high speed.

KNEADING BY HAND
Put the flour on a working surface or in a mixing bowl and make a large well in the center. Pour in the water. Mix until all the flour has been incorporated. Leave to rest for 1 hour, covered with a damp cloth, then incorporate the starter, fresh yeast, and salt. Knead the dough until it becomes smooth and elastic.

Shape the dough into a ball and cover with a damp cloth. Leave to rise for 1 hour 15 minutes. By the end of the rising time, the dough will have increased in volume.

Dust the work surface. Divide the dough into 2 equal pieces. Fold each piece over on itself, pulling gently to stretch into a longish log. Leave to rest for 30 minutes, covered with a damp cloth.

Working with 1 piece of dough at a time, use the palm of your hand to flatten it gently. With the long side facing you, fold in a third towards the center and press along the edge with the heel of your hand [1]. Swivel the dough 180 degrees [2]. Fold in the other long edge so that it overlaps in the center and press again. Fold one half on top of the other and seal the edges together with the heel of your hand [3]. With lightly floured hands, roll the dough out to 20 inches (50 cm) long [4]. Round off the ends. Repeat with the other loaf.

Place the loaves on a baking sheet lined with parchment (baking) paper, seams underneath. Cover with a damp cloth and leave to proof for 2 hours.

Place another baking sheet on the bottom shelf of the oven and preheat to 450°F (230°C). Slash each loaf 3 times lightly, in an oblique direction [5]. Just before putting the loaves in the oven, pour 50 g (scant ¼ cup) of water onto the preheated baking sheet. Bake for around 35 minutes.

Remove from the oven and leave to cool on a wire rack.

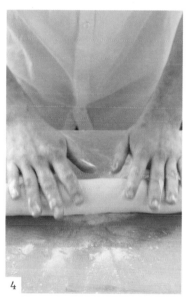

Traditional Breads

RUSTIC LOAF

Makes 3 loaves,
each about 300 g

TIMINGS
- Mixing & kneading: 9 min
- First rising: 1 h 30 min
- Resting: 30 min
- Proofing: 1 h 30 min
- Baking: 25 min

INGREDIENTS
- 400 g (3⅓ cups) all-purpose (plain) flour, plus extra for dusting
- 100 g (¾ cup) buckwheat flour
- 3 g (1 teaspooon) roasted malt (optional)
- 300 g (1¼ cups) water at 68°F (20°C)
- 100 g (scant ½ cup) liquid sourdough starter (or 25 g [3 tablespoons] dry sourdough starter)
- 2 g (½ teaspoon) fresh baker's yeast, crumbled
- 10 g (2 teaspoons) salt

KNEADING IN A STAND MIXER
Put all the ingredients in the bowl. Knead with the dough hook for 4 minutes at low speed, then for 5 minutes at high speed.

KNEADING BY HAND
Put the 2 flours and the roasted malt on the work surface or in a mixing bowl and make a large well in the center. Gradually pour in half the water [1], starter, fresh yeast, and salt. Mix well, then add the rest of the water and mix again until all the flour has been incorporated [2]. Knead the dough, pulling it up, slapping it forcefully down on the work surface, and folding it over on itself until it becomes smooth and elastic [3, 4].

Shape into a ball and cover with a damp cloth. Leave to rise for 1 hour 30 minutes.

Dust the work surface. Divide the dough into 3 equal pieces. Fold each piece over on itself, pulling gently to stretch into a longish log [5]. Cover with a damp cloth and leave to rest for 30 minutes.

Working with 1 piece of dough at a time, use the palm of your hand to flatten it gently. With the long side facing you, fold in a third towards the center and press along the edge with your fingertips. Swivel the dough 180 degrees. Fold in the other long edge so that it overlaps in the center and press again. Fold one half on top of the other and seal the edges together with the heel of your hand. With lightly floured hands, roll the dough out to form a plump oval. Shape the other 2 loaves the same way.

Place the loaves (seams underneath) on a baking sheet lined with parchment (baking) paper. Cover with a damp cloth and leave to proof for 1 hour 30 minutes.

Place another baking sheet on the bottom shelf of the oven and preheat to 475°F (240°C). Dust the loaves with a little all-purpose (plain) flour, then score each in a wide crisscross or diamond pattern [6]. Just before putting the loaves in the oven, pour 50 g (scant ¼ cup) of water onto the preheated baking sheet. Bake for around 25 minutes.

Remove from the oven and leave to cool on a wire rack.

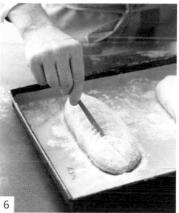

69

TABATIERE

Makes 3 loaves, each
about 300 g

TIMINGS
- Mixing & kneading: 16 min
- First resting: 1h
- First rising: 45 min
- Second resting: 30 min
- Proofing: 1h 30 min
- Baking: 20 min

INGREDIENTS
- 500 g (4 cups) all-purpose (plain) flour
- 325 g (scant 1⅓ cups) water at 68°F (20°C)
- 100 g (scant ½ cup) liquid sourdough starter (or 25 g [3 tablespoons] dry sourdough starter)
- 4 g (1⅓ teaspoons) fresh baker's yeast
- 10 g (2 teaspoons) salt
- rye flour for dusting

KNEADING IN A STAND MIXER
Put the flour and water in the bowl. Mix for 5 minutes at low speed. Remove the bowl from the machine and cover with a damp cloth. Leave to rest for 1 hour. Add the starter, fresh yeast, and salt. Knead with the dough hook for 4 minutes at low speed, then for 7 minutes at high speed.

KNEADING BY HAND
Put the flour on a work surface or in a mixing bowl and make a large well in the center. Pour in two-thirds of the water. Mix until all the flour is incorporated. Cover with a damp cloth and leave to rest for 1 hour. Add the remaining water, the starter, fresh yeast, and the salt. Knead the dough until it becomes smooth and elastic.

Shape the dough into a ball and cover with a damp cloth. Leave to rise for 45 minutes. It will have increased in volume by the end of the rising time.

Dust the work surface. Divide the dough into 3 equal pieces. Shape into balls, but don't work the dough too much. Cover with a damp cloth and leave to rest for 30 minutes.

Turn the balls so the seams are on top. Bring the edges to the center and press them down gently. Turn the dough over again and roll on the work surface, pressing gently, to form smooth, even-shaped balls. Dust with rye flour.

Use a rolling pin to flatten and roll a third of the dough out and away from you, creating a flap, around 6 inches (15 cm) long [1]. Dust lightly with rye flour, then bring the flap back over the top of the dough [2].

Place the loaves on a well-floured cloth, flaps underneath. Cover with a damp cloth and leave to proof for 1 hour 30 minutes.

Place a baking sheet on the bottom shelf of the oven and preheat to 450°F (230°C). Turn the dough onto another baking sheet lined with parchment (baking) paper or onto an oiled baking sheet [3]. The flap should now be on top. Score a leaf pattern. Just before putting the loaves in the oven, pour 50 g (scant ¼ cup) of water onto the preheated baking sheet. Bake for around 20 minutes.

Remove from the oven and let cool on a wire rack.

71   Traditional Breads

Tabatiere

Traditional Breads

SPLIT LOAF

Makes 3 loaves,
each about 300 g

TIMINGS

- Mixing & kneading: 16 min
- First resting: 1h
- First rising: 1h
- Second resting:
  30 min + 20 min
- Proofing: 1h 20 min
- Baking: 20 min

INGREDIENTS

- 500 g (4 cups) all-purpose (plain) flour
- 300 g (1¼ cups) water at 68°F (20°C)
- 100 g (scant ½ cup) liquid sourdough starter (or 25 g [3 tablespoons] dry sourdough starter)
- 4 g (1⅓ teaspoons) fresh baker's yeast
- 10 g (2 teaspoons) salt
- Rye flour for dusting

KNEADING IN A STAND MIXER

Put the flour and water in the bowl. Mix for 5 minutes at low speed. Remove the bowl from the machine and cover with a damp cloth. Leave to rest for 1 hour. Add the starter, fresh yeast, and salt. Knead with the dough hook for 4 minutes at low speed, then for 7 minutes at high speed.

KNEADING BY HAND

Put the flour on a work surface or in a mixing bowl and make a large well in the center. Pour in two-thirds of the water. Mix until all the flour is incorporated. Cover with a damp cloth and leave to rest for 1 hour. Add the rest of the water, the starter, fresh yeast, and salt. Knead the dough until it becomes smooth and elastic.

Shape the dough into a ball and cover with a damp cloth. Leave to rise for 1 hour. It will have increased in volume by the end of the rising time.

Dust the work surface. Divide the dough into 3 equal pieces. Shape into balls, but don't work the dough too much. Cover with a damp cloth and leave to rest for 30 minutes.

Working with 1 ball of dough at a time, use the palm of your hand to flatten it gently [1]. Fold in a third towards the center and press with the heel of your hand [2]. Swivel the dough 180 degrees [3]. Fold in the other edge so that it overlaps in the center and press again. Fold one half on top of the other and seal the edges together with the heel of your hand [4]. With lightly floured hands, roll the dough out to form a plump oval. Shape the other 2 balls of dough the same way. Leave to rest for 20 minutes.

Dust the loaves with rye flour. Use a rolling pin to press into each loaf along its length [5], then bring the edges together [6].

Turn the loaves onto a well-floured baker's cloth, split sides underneath. Cover with a damp cloth and leave to proof for 1 hour 20 minutes.

Place a baking sheet on the bottom shelf of the oven and preheat to 450°F (230°C). Turn the dough, split sides on top, onto another baking sheet lined with parchment (baking) paper. Just before putting the loaves in the oven, pour 50 g (scant ¼ cup) of water onto the preheated baking sheet. Bake for 20 minutes.

Remove from the oven and let cool on a wire rack.

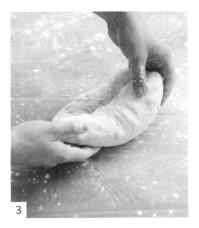

Traditional Breads

DAISY LOAF

Makes 2 loaves,
each about 470 g

TIMINGS
• Mixing & kneading: 11 min
• First rising: 1h
• Resting: 15 min
• Proofing: 1h 30 min
• Baking: 25 min

INGREDIENTS
• 50 g (1/2 cup) rye flour
• 450 g (3 3/4 cups)
  all-purpose (plain) flour,
  plus extra for dusting
• 320 g (generous 1 1/4 cups)
  water at 68°F (20°C)
• 100 g (scant 1/2 cup)
  liquid sourdough starter
  (or 25 g [3 tablespoons]
  dry sourdough starter)
• 4 g (1 1/3 teaspoons)
  fresh baker's yeast
• 10 g (2 teaspoons) salt

KNEADING IN A STAND MIXER
Put the 2 flours, water, starter, yeast, and salt in the bowl. Knead with the dough hook for 4 minutes at low speed, then for 7 minutes at high speed.

KNEADING BY HAND
Put the 2 flours on the work surface or in a mixing bowl and make a large well in the center. Pour in half the water, the starter, fresh yeast, and salt. Mix well, then add the remaining water and mix until all the flour is incorporated. Knead the dough until it becomes smooth and elastic.

Shape the dough into a ball and cover with a damp cloth. Leave to rise for 1 hour. Midway through the rise, deflate the dough by folding it in half. By the end of the rising time, it will have increased in volume.

Dust the work surface. Divide the dough into 14 equal pieces. Gently roll them into balls under your hands [1]. Cover with a damp cloth and leave to rest for 15 minutes.

Roll the balls again. Arrange them on baking sheets lined with parchment (baking) paper to form daisy shapes. For each daisy, arrange 6 balls around a central one, seams underneath [2]. (You can seal the balls together by moistening them at the point where they meet but it is not essential.) Flour the loaves [3]. Cover with a damp cloth and leave to proof for 1 hour 30 minutes.

Place a baking sheet on the bottom shelf of the oven and preheat to 450°F (230°C). Just before putting the loaves in the oven, pour 50 g (scant 1/4 cup) of water onto the preheated baking sheet. Bake for 10 minutes, then lower the temperature to 410°F (210°C) and bake for another 15 minutes.

Remove from the oven [4] and leave to cool on a wire rack.

Traditional Breads

PORTE-MANTEAU

Makes 3 loaves,
each about 300 g

TIMINGS
- Mixing & kneading: 15 min
- First resting: 1h
- First rising: 1h 30 min
- Second resting: 30 min
- Proofing: 1h 40 min
- Baking: 20 min

INGREDIENTS
- 500 g (4 cups) all-purpose (plain) flour, plus extra for dusting
- 325 g (generous 1¼ cups) water at 68°F (20°C)
- 100 g (scant ½ cup) liquid sourdough starter (or 25 g [3 tablespoons] dry sourdough starter)
- 3 g (1 teaspoon) fresh baker's yeast
- 10 g (2 teaspoons) salt

KNEADING IN A STAND MIXER
Put the flour and water in the bowl. Mix for 4 minutes at low speed. Remove the bowl from the machine and cover with a damp cloth. Leave to rest for 1 hour. Add the starter, fresh yeast, and salt. Knead with the dough hook for 4 minutes at low speed, then for 7 minutes at high speed.

KNEADING BY HAND
Put the flour on a work surface or in a mixing bowl and make a large well in the center. Pour in two-thirds of the water and mix until all the flour is incorporated. Cover with a damp cloth and leave to rest for 1 hour. Add the rest of the water, the starter, fresh yeast, and salt. Knead the dough until it becomes smooth and elastic.

Shape the dough into a ball and cover with a damp cloth. Leave to rise for 1 hour 30 minutes. It will have increased in volume by the end of the rising time.

Dust the work surface. Divide the dough into 3 equal pieces. Fold each piece over on itself, pulling gently to lengthen. Cover with a damp cloth and leave to rest for 30 minutes.

Working with 1 piece of dough at a time, use the palm of your hand to flatten it gently into a rough oval. With the long side facing you, fold in a third towards the center and press along the edge with your fingertips. Swivel the dough 180 degrees. Fold in the other long edge so that it overlaps in the center and press again. Fold one half on top of the other and seal the edges together with the heel of your hand. With lightly floured hands, roll the dough out to form a "baguette," around 22 inches (55 cm) long. Shape the other 2 loaves the same way.

Visually divide each baguette into 3 and flatten the two outer thirds, starting from the center and working out to the edge [1]. Roll in the thinner outer sections to the center [2], 1 side at a time [3, 4]. To form the final higher shape, roll up 1 side slightly more than the other.

Turn the loaves, rolled sides down, onto a baking sheet lined with parchment (baking) paper [5, 6]. Cover with a damp cloth and leave to proof for 1 hour 40 minutes, by which time they will have increased in volume [7].

Place another baking sheet on the bottom shelf of the oven and preheat to 450°F (230°C). Invert the loaves so the rolled side is on top [8]. Just before putting the loaves in the oven, pour 50 g (scant ¼ cup) of water onto the preheated baking sheet. Bake for 20 minutes.

Remove from the oven and leave to cool on a wire rack.

1

2

3

4

5

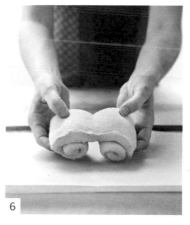

6

7

8

Traditional Breads

THE TWIST

Makes 3 loaves,
each about 300 g

TIMINGS
- Mixing & kneading: 10 min
- First rising: 1 h 30 min
- Resting: 50 min
- Proofing: 1 h 30 min
- Baking: 20 min

INGREDIENTS
- 500 g (4 cups) all-purpose (plain) flour, plus extra for dusting and dusting
- 310 g (scant 1¼ cups) water at 68°F (20°C)
- 100 g (scant ½ cup) liquid sourdough starter (or 25 g [3 tablespoons] dry sourdough starter)
- 4 g (1⅓ teaspoons) fresh baker's yeast
- 10 g (2 teaspoons) salt

KNEADING IN A STAND MIXER
Put the flour, water, starter, yeast, and salt in the bowl. Knead with the dough hook for 4 minutes at low speed, then for 6 minutes at high speed.

KNEADING BY HAND
Put the flour on a work surface or in a mixing bowl and make a large well in the center. Pour in half the water, the starter, fresh yeast, and salt. Mix well, then add the remaining water and mix until all the flour is incorporated. Knead the dough until it becomes smooth and elastic.

Shape the dough into a ball and cover with a damp cloth. Leave to rise for 1 hour 30 minutes. The dough will have increased in volume at the end of the rising time.

Dust the work surface. Divide the dough into 3 equal pieces. Fold each piece over on itself, pulling gently to lengthen. Cover with a damp cloth and leave to rest for 30 minutes.

Working with 1 piece of dough at a time, use the palm of your hand to flatten it gently. With the long side facing you, fold in a third towards the center and press along the edge with your fingertips. Swivel the dough 180 degrees. Fold in the other long edge so that it overlaps in the center and press again. Fold one half on top of the other and seal the edges together with the heel of your hand.

With lightly floured hands, roll the dough out to around 16 inches (40 cm). Shape the other loaves in the same way. Leave to rest for 20 minutes.

Dust the loaves with flour. Use a rolling pin to press into each loaf along its length [1], then bring the edges together [2]. Pick up the ends of the dough and twist gently. Keep 1 hand still while you twist 3 times with the other; do this in stages, resting between each twist in order to achieve a neat finish [3, 4, 5].

Arrange the loaves on a baking sheet lined with parchment (baking) paper. Cover with a damp cloth and leave to proof for 1 hour 30 minutes.

Place another baking sheet on the bottom shelf of the oven and preheat to 450°F (230°C). Invert the loaves so the rolled side is on top. Just before putting the loaves in the oven, pour 50 g (scant ¼ cup) of water onto the preheated baking sheet. Bake for 20 minutes.

Remove from the oven and let cool on a wire rack.

1

2

3

4

5

Traditional Breads

ZIGZAG BREAD

Makes 2 loaves,
each about 425 g

TIMINGS
• Mixing & kneading: 10 min
• First rising: 1h30 min
• Resting: 45 min
• Proofing: 1h30 min
• Baking: 25 min

INGREDIENTS
• 50 g (½ cup) rye flour,
  plus extra for dusting
• 450 g (3¾ cups)
  all-purpose (plain) flour
• 320 g (generous 1¼ cups)
  water at 68°F (20°C)
• 100 g (scant ½ cup)
  liquid sourdough starter
  (or 25 g [3 tablespoons]
  dry sourdough starter)
• 4 g (1⅓ teaspoons) fresh
  baker's yeast
• 10 g (2 teaspoons) salt

KNEADING IN A STAND MIXER
Put the 2 flours, water, starter, yeast, and salt in the bowl. Knead with the dough hook for 4 minutes at low speed, then for 6 minutes at high speed.

KNEADING BY HAND
Put the 2 flours on the work surface or in a mixing bowl and make a large well in the center. Pour in half the water, the starter, fresh yeast, and salt. Mix well, then add the remaining water and mix until all the flour is incorporated. Knead the dough until it becomes smooth and elastic.

Shape the dough into a ball and cover with a damp cloth. Leave to rise for 1 hour 30 minutes. Midway through the rise, deflate the dough by folding it in half. By the end of the rising time it will have increased in volume.

Dust the work surface. Divide the dough into 2 equal pieces. Shape into balls, but don't work the dough too much. Cover with a damp cloth and leave to rest for 45 minutes.

Working with 1 piece of dough at a time, use the palm of your hand to flatten it gently to a rough oval. With the long side facing you, fold in a third towards the center and press along the edge with your fingertips. Swivel the dough 180 degrees. Fold in the other long edge so that it overlaps in the center and press again. Fold one half on top of the other and seal the edges together with the heel of your hand.

Flatten the loaves with your hands again and dust with flour. Using a dough cutter (lame), score 8 very deep cuts in a crosshatch pattern (4 inches each direction), taking care not to cut right through the dough.

Turn the loaves over onto a floured baker's cloth. Cover with another damp cloth and leave to proof for 1 hour 30 minutes.

Place a baking sheet on the bottom shelf of the oven and preheat to 450°F (230°C). Invert the loaves onto another baking sheet lined with parchment (baking) paper, scored surface on top. Just before putting the loaves in the oven, pour 50 g (scant ¼ cup) of water onto the preheated baking sheet. Bake for 10 minutes, then lower the temperature to 410°F (210°C) and continue baking for another 15 minutes.

Remove from the oven and leave to cool on a wire rack.

COURONNE BREAD RING

Makes 1 crown, about 930 g

TIMINGS
- Mixing & kneading: 11 min
- First rising: 1 h
- Resting time: 45 min
- Proofing: 1 h 30 min
- Baking: 25 min

INGREDIENTS
- 50 g (½ cup) rye flour, plus extra for dusting
- 450 g (3¾ cups) all-purpose (plain) flour, plus extra for dusting
- 320 g (generous 1¼ cups) water at 68°F (20°C)
- 100 g (scant ½ cup) liquid sourdough starter (or 25 g [3 tablespoons] dry sourdough starter)
- 4 g (1⅓ teaspoons) fresh baker's yeast
- 10 g (2 teaspoons) salt

KNEADING IN A STAND MIXER
Put the 2 flours, the water, starter, yeast, and salt in the bowl. Knead with the dough hook for 4 minutes at low speed, then for 7 minutes at high speed.

KNEADING BY HAND
Put the 2 flours on the work surface or in a mixing bowl and make a large well in the center. Pour in half the water, then add the starter, fresh yeast, and salt. Mix well, then add the remaining water and mix until all the flour is incorporated. Knead the dough until it becomes smooth and elastic.

Shape the dough into a ball and cover with a damp cloth. Leave to rise for 1 hour. Midway through the rise, deflate the dough by folding it in half. By the end of the rising time, it will have increased in volume.

Dust the work surface. Divide the dough into 6 equal pieces portions. Roll into balls, then cover with a damp cloth and leave to rest for 45 minutes.

Roll the dough pieces on the work surface, pressing gently, to form smooth, even-shaped balls [1]. Dust with flour. Working with 1 piece at a time, use a rolling pin to flatten and roll a third of the dough out and away from you, creating a flap [2], around 3¼ inches (8 cm) long. Dust lightly with flour [3], then bring the flap back over the top of the dough [4]. Shape the other dough balls the same way.

Place the dough balls, flaps underneath, in a floured banneton ring (known as a *couronne*) [5]. They should be just touching, so that they merge on rising to form the traditional crown shape. Cover with a damp cloth and leave to proof for 1 hour 30 minutes.

Place a baking sheet on the bottom shelf of the oven and preheat to 450°F (230°C). Gently turn the crown out onto another baking sheet lined with parchment (baking) paper. The flaps should now be on top. Just before putting the crown in the oven, pour 50 g (scant ¼ cup) of water onto the preheated baking sheet. Bake for 10 minutes, then lower the temperature to 410°F (210°C) and continue baking for another 15 minutes.

Remove from the oven and leave to cool on a wire rack.

Couronne Bread Ring   88

Traditional Breads

BOW TIE BREAD

Makes 2 loaves,
each about 450 g

TIMINGS
• Mixing & kneading: 11 min
• First rising: 2 h
• Resting: 15 min + 20 min
• Proofing: 1 h 20 min
• Baking: 25 min

INGREDIENTS
• 50 g (½ cup) rye flour
• 450 g (3¾ cups) all-
  purpose (plain) flour,
  plus extra for dusting
• 300 g (1¼ cups) water
  at 68°F (20°C)
• 100 g (scant ½ cup)
  liquid sourdough starter
  (or 25 g [3 tablespoons]
  dry sourdough starter)
• 4 g (1⅓ teaspoons)
  fresh baker's yeast
• 10 g (2 teaspoons) salt

KNEADING IN A STAND MIXER
Put the 2 flours, water, starter, yeast, and salt in the bowl. Knead with the dough hook for 4 minutes at low speed, then for 7 minutes at high speed.

KNEADING BY HAND
Put the 2 flours on the work surface or in a mixing bowl and make a large well in the center. Pour in half the water, the starter, fresh yeast, and salt. Mix well, then add the remaining water and mix until all the flour is incorporated. Knead the dough until it becomes smooth and elastic.

Shape the dough into a ball and cover with a damp cloth. Leave to rise for 2 hours. Midway through the rise, deflate the dough by folding it in half. By the end of the rising time it will have increased in volume.

Dust the work surface. Divide the dough into 2 equal pieces and shape into balls. Cover with a damp cloth and leave to rest for 15 minutes.

Turn the balls over so the seams are on top. Bring the edges to the center and press them down gently. Turn the dough over again and roll on the work surface, pressing gently, to form smooth, even-shaped balls. Cover with a damp cloth and leave to rest for 20 minutes. Dust with flour.

Use a rolling pin to flatten and roll a third of the dough out and away from you, creating a flap around 6 inches (15 cm) long. Dust lightly with flour, then bring the flap back over the top of the dough. Shape the other loaf in the same way.

Place the loaves on a well-floured baker's cloth, flaps underneath. Cover with a damp cloth and leave to proof for 1 hour 20 minutes.

Place a baking sheet on the bottom shelf of the oven and preheat to 450°F (230°C). Turn the loaves onto another baking sheet lined with parchment (baking) paper. The flaps should now be on top. Use a dough cutter (lame) to make a 2-inch (5-cm) cut right through each loaf, to create 2 "wings."

Dust each loaf with flour and score with your favorite pattern. Just before putting the loaves in the oven, pour 50 g (scant ¼ cup) of water onto the preheated baking sheet. Bake for 25 minutes.

Remove from the oven and leave to cool on a wire rack.

SPECIALTY BREADS

"FIRST MILL" LOAF

Makes 3 loaves,
each about 330 g

TIMINGS
- Mixing & kneading:
  12 1/2 min
- First rising: 2 h
- Resting: 30 min
- Proofing: 2 h
- Baking: 25 min

INGREDIENTS
- 400 g (3 1/3 cups)
  all-purpose (plain) flour
- 75 g (1/2 cup plus
  2 tablespoons) "first
  mill" flour
- 25 g (1/4 cup) coarse
  rye flour
- 100 g (scant 1/2 cup)
  liquid sourdough starter
  (or 25 g [3 tablespoons]
  dry sourdough starter)
- 1 g (1/3 teaspoon) fresh
  baker's yeast, crumbled
- 10 g (2 teaspoons) sea salt
- 360 g (scant 1 1/2 cups)
  warm water at 82.4-86°F
  (28-30°C) [1]
- 10 g (2 teaspoons)
  grapeseed oil

"First mill" or "first break" flours, known as *farines du premier broyage* in French, are made during the first grinding process where the wheat is partially torn and some of the endosperm is reduced to a flour.

KNEADING IN A STAND MIXER
Put the 3 flours, starter, fresh yeast, and sea salt in the bowl. Add three-quarters of the water and knead with the dough hook at low speed for 12 minutes. When the dough is quite smooth, add the remaining water and the grapeseed oil and knead for 30 seconds at high speed.

KNEADING BY HAND
Put the 3 flours on a work surface or in a mixing bowl and make a large well in the center. Pour in half the water, then add the starter, fresh yeast, and sea salt. Mix well, then gradually add the rest of the water and the grapeseed oil and blend until all the flour has been incorporated. Knead the dough until it becomes smooth and elastic.

Shape into a ball and cover with a damp cloth [2]. Leave to rise for 2 hours. Midway through the rise, deflate the dough by folding it in half. By the end of the rising time, it will have increased in volume [3].

Dust the work surface. Divide the dough into 3 equal pieces [4], and shape them into balls. Cover with a damp cloth and leave to rest for 30 minutes.

Working with 1 piece of dough at a time, use the palm of your hand to flatten it gently. Fold 1 long side in so that it overlaps the center. Fold the remaining side on top and seal the edges together with your fingertips [5]. Shape the other 2 loaves in the same way.

Place the loaves on a floured baker's cloth, seams underneath. Separate them by making folds in the cloth. Cover with a damp cloth and leave to proof for 2 hours.

Place a baking sheet on the bottom shelf of the oven and preheat to 450°F (230°C). Turn out the loaves onto another baking sheet lined with parchment (baking) paper, seams on top. Just before putting them in the oven, pour 50 g (scant 1/4 cup) of water onto the preheated baking sheet. Bake for 25 minutes.

Remove from the oven and leave to cool on a wire rack.

95

CORNMEAL LOAF

Makes 3 loaves,
each about 300 g

TIMINGS
- Mixing & kneading: 10 min
- First rising: 45 min
- Resting: 30 min
- Proofing: 1 h 20 min
- Baking: 25 min

INGREDIENTS
- 300 g (2½ cups)
  all-purpose (plain) flour
- 200 g (1¼) cups
  fine cornmeal
- 320 g (generous 1¼ cups)
  water at 68°F (20°C)
- 100 g (scant ½ cup)
  liquid sourdough starter
  (or 25 g [2 tablespoons]
  dry sourdough starter)
- 3 g (1 teaspoon) fresh
  baker's yeast, crumbled
- 10 g (2 teaspoons) salt

KNEADING IN A STAND MIXER
Put the flour, water, cornmeal, starter [1], fresh yeast, and salt in the bowl. Knead with the dough hook for 4 minutes at low speed [2], then for 6 minutes at high speed [3].

KNEADING BY HAND
Put the bread flour and cornmeal on a work surface or in a mixing bowl and make a large well in the center. Pour in half the water, then add the starter, fresh yeast, and salt. Mix well, then add the rest of the water and blend until all the flour has been incorporated. Knead the dough until it becomes smooth and elastic.

Shape into a ball and cover with a damp cloth. Leave to rise for 45 minutes. The dough will have increased in volume by the end of the rising time.

Dust the work surface. Divide the dough into 3 equal pieces and shape them into balls [4]. Cover with a damp cloth and leave to rest for 30 minutes.

Working with 1 piece of dough at a time, use the palm of your hand to flatten it gently into a rough oval. With the long side facing you, fold in a third towards the center [5] and press along the edge with the heel of your hand [6]. Swivel the dough 180 degrees. Fold in the other long edge so that it overlaps in the center and press again [7]. Fold one half on top of the other and seal the edges together with the heel of your hand [8, 9]. With lightly floured hands, roll the dough out to form a plump oval [10]. Shape the other 2 loaves the same way.

Place the loaves on a baking sheet lined with parchment (baking) paper, seams underneath. Cover with a damp cloth and leave to proof for 1 hour 20 minutes.

Place another baking sheet on the bottom shelf of the oven and preheat to 450°F (230°C). Before baking, score each loaf 5 times lengthwise, starting in the middle and working out [11]. Just before putting the loaves in the oven, pour 50 g (scant ¼ cup) of water onto the preheated baking sheet. Bake for 25 minutes.

Remove from the oven and leave to cool on a wire rack.

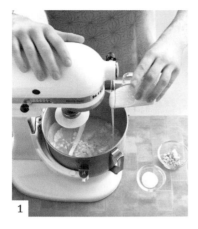  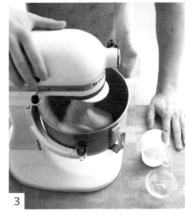

 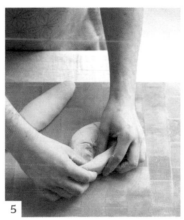 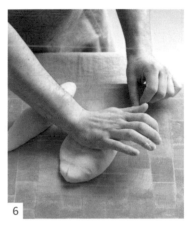

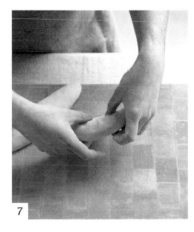 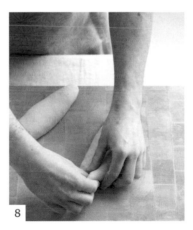 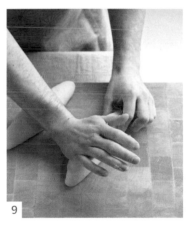

 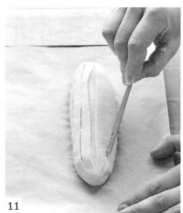 

Specialty Breads

MIXED SEED BREAD

Makes 3 loaves,
each about 350 g

TIMINGS
- Mixing & kneading:
  10 min + 2h soaking
- First rising: 1h 30 min
- Resting: 15 min
- Proofing: 2h
- Baking: 20-25 min

INGREDIENTS
- 90 g (generous ½ cup)
  mixed seeds (flax, poppy,
  sesame, millet, quinoa),
  plus extra for topping
- 500 g (4 cups) all-purpose
  (plain) flour, plus extra
  for dusting
- 300 g (1¼ cups) water
  at 68°F (20°C), plus 60 g
  (¼ cup) for steeping the
  seeds
- 100 g (scant ½ cup)
  liquid sourdough starter
  (or 25 g [2 tablespoons]
  dry sourdough starter)
- 3 g (1 teaspoon) fresh
  baker's yeast, crumbled
- 10 g (2 teaspoons) salt

Preheat the oven to 480°F (250°C). Spread the seeds out on a baking sheet lined with parchment (baking) paper and toast for 10 minutes. Tip them immediately into a bowl with the 60 g (2¼ cup) water and leave to steep for around 2 hours. Drain away any water that remains.

KNEADING IN A STAND MIXER
Put the flour, water, starter, fresh yeast, and salt in the bowl. Knead with the dough hook for 4 minutes at low speed, then for 6 minutes at high speed. Add the toasted seeds and mix in briefly.

KNEADING BY HAND
Put the flour on a work surface or in a mixing bowl and make a large well in the center. Pour in half the water, the starter, fresh yeast, and salt. Mix well, then add the remaining water and the toasted seeds, and blend until all the flour is incorporated. Knead the dough until it becomes smooth and elastic.

Shape into a ball and cover with a damp cloth. Leave to rise for 1 hour 30 minutes. The dough will have increased in volume by the end of the rising time.

Dust the work surface. Divide the dough into 3 equal pieces and shape them into balls. Cover with a damp cloth and leave to rest for 15 minutes.

Working with 1 piece of dough at a time, use the palm of your hand to flatten it gently into a rough oval. With the long side facing you, fold in a third towards the center and press along the edge with the heel of your hand. Swivel the dough 180 degrees. Fold in the other long edge so that it overlaps in the center and press again. Fold one half on top of the other and seal the edges together with the heel of your hand. With lightly floured hands, roll the dough out to form a plump oval. Shape the other 2 loaves the same way.

Cover a plate with extra mixed seeds. Moisten the dough pieces by spraying or brushing them lightly with water. Roll the top of each loaf in the seeds then immediately place on a baking sheet lined with parchment (baking) paper, seams underneath. Cover with a damp cloth and leave to proof for 2 hours.

Place another baking sheet on the bottom shelf of the oven and preheat to 450°F (230°C). Score each loaf lengthwise (see page 40). Just before putting the loaves in the oven, pour 50 g (scant ¼ cup) of water onto the preheated baking sheet. Bake for 20-25 minutes.

Remove from the oven and leave to cool on a wire rack.

KAMUT®
BREAD

Makes 3 loaves,
each about 320 g

TIMINGS
- Mixing & kneading: 8 min
- First rising: 1 h 30 min
- Resting: 30 min
- Proofing: 1 h 30 min
- Baking: 25 min

INGREDIENTS
- 300 g (2 1/2 cups)
  Kamut® flour
  (Khorasan wheat flour)
- 200 g (1 2/3 cups) organic
  all-purpose (plain) flour
- 300 g (1 1/4 cups) water
  at 68°F (20°C)
- 150 g (2/3 cup) liquid
  sourdough starter (or 30 g
  [3 1/3 tablespoons] dry
  sourdough starter)
- 1 g (1/3 teaspoon) fresh
  baker's yeast, crumbled
- 10 g (2 teaspoons) salt

KNEADING IN A STAND MIXER
Put the 2 flours, water, starter, fresh yeast, and salt in the bowl. Knead with the dough hook for 4 minutes at low speed, then for 4 minutes at high speed.

KNEADING BY HAND
Put the 2 flours on a work surface or in a mixing bowl [1] and make a large well in the center. Pour in half the water, then add the starter, fresh yeast, and salt. Mix well [2], then add the rest of the water and blend until all the flour has been incorporated. Knead the dough until it becomes smooth and elastic.

Shape into a ball and cover with a damp cloth. Leave to rise for 1 hour 30 minutes, by which time the dough will have increased in volume [3].

Dust the work surface. Divide the dough into 3 equal pieces [4] and shape them into batons. Cover with a damp cloth and leave to rest for 30 minutes.

Working with 1 piece of dough at a time, use the palm of your hand to flatten it gently into a rough oval. With the long side facing you, fold in a third towards the center and press along the edge with your fingertips [5]. Swivel the dough 180 degrees. Fold in the other long edge so that it overlaps in the center and press again [6]. Fold one half on top of the other and seal the edges together with the heel of your hand. With lightly floured hands, roll the dough out to form a thick log, about 8 inches (20 cm) [7]. Shape the other 2 loaves the same way.

Place the loaves on a baking sheet lined with parchment (baking) paper, seams underneath. Cover with a damp cloth and leave to proof for 1 hour 30 minutes.

Place another baking sheet on the bottom shelf of the oven and preheat to 450°F (230°C). Lightly dust the loaves with Kamut® flour [8]. Score each loaf twice [9]. Just before putting the loaves in the oven, pour 50 g (scant 1/4 cup) of water onto the preheated baking sheet. Bake for 25 minutes.

Remove from the oven and leave to cool on a wire rack.

△ Kamut® flour (see page 102) is tricky to work with and doesn't rise very much. For the best chance of success, try baking the bread in a mold or loaf pan on your first attempt.

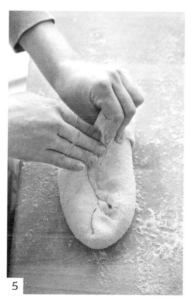

101   Specialty Breads

KAMUT®

Kamut® is a wheat species that is both modern and ancient. The story goes that, during the 1950s, an American airman in Egypt came upon some unusually large grains of wheat.
He sent some to a friend whose father was a farmer in Montana as he was curious to know what type of wheat these grains would produce. The farmer was quick to sow the wheat and achieved a successful first crop, to which he gave the encouraging name of "King Tut's wheat." Around 30 years later, an agronomic engineer called Bob Quinn began to market this wheat under the name Kamut®, which means "wheat" in ancient Egyptian. Kamut® is a hard wheat related to the Khorasan wheat variety that has existed since antiquity throughout the Fertile Crescent , the historical region that includes Iraq, Kuwait, and parts of Iran and Turkey, as well as Cyprus and the Levantine coast of the Mediterranean. Its spectacular growth in production in recent years is due to its exceptional nutritional value.

WHOLE WHEAT BREAD

Makes 3 loaves,
each about 325 g

TIMINGS
- Mixing & kneading: 10 min
- First rising: 1 h
- Resting: 15 min
- Proofing: 1 h 30 min
- Baking: 25 min

INGREDIENTS
- 500 g (4 cups) whole wheat flour, plus extra for dusting
- 360 g (scant 1½ cups) water at 68°F (20°C)
- 100 g (scant ½ cup) liquid sourdough starter (or 25 g [2 tablespoons] dry sourdough starter)
- 3 g (1 teaspoon) fresh baker's yeast, crumbled
- 10 g (2 teaspoons) salt

KNEADING IN A STAND MIXER
Put all the ingredients in the bowl. Knead with the dough hook for 4 minutes at low speed, then for 6 minutes at high speed.

KNEADING BY HAND
Put the flour on a work surface or in a mixing bowl and make a large hole in the center. Pour in half the water, starter, fresh yeast, and salt. Mix well, then add the rest of the water and blend [1] until all the flour has been incorporated. Knead the dough until it becomes smooth and elastic.

Shape into a ball and cover with a damp cloth. Leave to rise for 1 hour. By the end of the rising time, the dough will have increased in volume.

Dust the work surface. Divide the dough into 3 equal pieces and shape each into a ball. Cover with a damp cloth and leave to rest for 15 minutes [2].

Working with 1 piece of dough at a time, use the palm of your hand to flatten it gently into a rough oval. With the long side facing you, fold in a third towards the center and press along the edge with your fingertips. Swivel the dough 180 degrees. Fold in the other long edge so that it overlaps in the center and press with the heel of your hand [3]. Fold one half on top of the other, and seal the edges together with the heel of your hand. With lightly floured hands, roll the dough out to form a plump oval. Shape the other 2 loaves the same way.

Place the loaves on a baking sheet lined with parchment (baking) paper, seams underneath. Score the loaves in a "sausage" cut (page 41) [4]. Cover with a damp cloth and leave to proof for 1 hour 30 minutes. The incisions will stretch and widen as the dough rises [5].

Place another baking sheet on the bottom shelf of the oven and preheat to 450°F (230°C). Just before putting the loaves in the oven, pour 50 g (scant ¼ cup) of water onto the preheated baking sheet. Bake for 25 minutes.

Remove from the oven and leave to cool on a wire rack.

△ If you prefer a lighter loaf, use a mix of equal parts whole wheat and all-purpose (plain) flour.

1

2

3

4

5

Specialty Breads

SEMOLINA BREAD

Makes 2 loaves,
each about 470 g

TIMINGS

- Mixing & kneading: 11 min
- First rising: 2h
- Resting: 15 min
- Proofing: 2h
- Baking: 20 min

INGREDIENTS

- 375 g (3 cups) all-purpose (plain) flour
- 125 g (¾ cup) fine semolina flour
- 100 g (scant ½ cup) liquid sourdough starter (or 25 g [2 tablespoons] dry sourdough starter)
- 325 g (1⅓ cups) water at 68°F (20°C)
- 2 g (½ teaspoon) fresh baker's yeast, crumbled
- 10 g (2 teaspoons) salt

KNEADING IN A STAND MIXER

Put all the ingredients in the bowl [1] and knead with the dough hook for 4 minutes at low speed, then for 7 minutes at high speed.

KNEADING BY HAND

Put the 2 flours on a work surface or in a bowl and make a large well in the center. Pour in half the water, the starter, fresh yeast, and salt. Mix well, add the remaining water, and blend until all the flour has been incorporated. Knead well until the dough becomes smooth and elastic.

Shape into a ball and place in a banneton dusted with semolina flour [2]. Cover with a damp cloth and leave to rise for 2 hours. By the end of the rising time, the dough will have increased in volume [3].

Dust the work surface. Divide the dough into 2 equal pieces and shape them into balls. Cover with a damp cloth and leave to rest for 15 minutes.

Working with 1 piece of dough at a time, use the palm of your hand to flatten it gently into a rough oval. With the long side facing you, fold in a third towards the center and press along the edge with your fingertips [4]. Swivel the dough 180 degrees [5]. Dust with semolina flour [6] then fold the other long edge on top and seal the edges together with your fingertips [7]. Shape the other loaf the same way.

Place the loaves, seams underneath, on a floured baker's cloth, separated by a fold [8]. Cover with a damp cloth and leave to proof for 2 hours.

Place a baking sheet on the bottom shelf of the oven and preheat to 450°F (230°C). Carefully turn the loaves onto another baking sheet lined with parchment (baking) paper, seams on top. Just before putting the loaves in the oven pour 50 g (scant ¼ cup) of water onto the preheated baking sheet. Bake for 20 minutes. The loaves will split along the seams.

Remove from the oven and leave to cool on a wire rack.

△ Take care not to overcook this loaf; the crust should be light and crisp.

COUNTRY LOAF

Makes 1 loaf,
about 950 g

TIMINGS
- Mixing & kneading: 11min
- First rising: 2h
- Resting: 30min
- Proofing: 1h30min
- Baking: 25min

INGREDIENTS
- 50 g (scant ½ cup) rye flour
- 450 g (3¾ cups) all-purpose (plain) flour
- 340 g (generous 1⅓ cups) water at 68°F (20°C)
- 100 g (scant ½ cup) liquid sourdough starter (or 25 g [2 tablespoons] dry sourdough starter)
- 2 g (½ teaspoon) fresh baker's yeast, crumbled
- 10 g (2 teaspoons) salt

KNEADING IN A STAND MIXER
Put all the ingredients in the bowl. Knead with the dough hook for 4 minutes at low speed, then for 7 minutes at high speed.

KNEADING BY HAND
Put the 2 flours on a work surface or in a mixing bowl and make a large well in the center. Pour in half the water, then add the starter, fresh yeast, and salt. Mix well [1], then add the rest of the water and blend until all the flour has been incorporated. Next, knead the dough and fold it energetically [2, 3] until it becomes smooth and elastic.

Shape the dough into a ball [4] and cover with a damp cloth. Leave to rise for 2 hours. Midway through the rise, deflate the dough by folding it in half. By the end of the rising time it will have increased in volume.

Carefully shape it into a ball again and leave to rest for 30 minutes, covered with a damp cloth.

Working with 1 piece of dough at a time, use the palm of your hand to flatten it gently into a rough oval. With the long side facing you, fold in a third towards the center and press along the edge with your fingertips [5]. Swivel the dough 180 degrees. Fold in the other long edge so that it overlaps in the center and press with the heel of your hand. Fold one half on top of the other, and seal the edges together with the heel of your hand [6]. With lightly floured hands, roll the dough out to form a plump oval. Shape the other 2 loaves the same way [7].

Place the loaf, seam uppermost, on a floured baker's cloth. Leave to proof for 1 hour 30 minutes, covered with a damp cloth.

Place a baking sheet on the bottom shelf of the oven and preheat to 450°F (230°C). Turn the loaf onto another baking sheet lined with parchment (baking) paper, with the seam underneath. Score it once lengthwise [8] or twice across the width.

Just before putting the loaf in the oven, pour 50 g (scant ¼ cup) of water onto the preheated baking sheet. Bake for 10 minutes, then lower the temperature to 410°F (210°C) and bake for another 15 minutes.

Remove from the oven and leave to cool on a wire rack.

Specialty Breads

BRAN LOAF

Makes 1 loaf, about 930 g

TIMINGS
- Mixing & kneading: 10 min
- First rising: 45 min
- Resting: 30 min
- Proofing: 1 h 30 min
- Baking: 20–25 min

INGREDIENTS
- 150 g (3 cups) wheat bran
- 300 g (2½ cups) all-purpose (plain) flour
- 50 g (½ cup) rye flour
- 320 g (generous 1¼ cups) water at 68°F (20°C)
- 100 g (scant ½ cup) liquid sourdough starter (or 25 g [2 tablespoons] dry sourdough starter)
- 3 g (1 teaspoon) fresh baker's yeast, crumbled
- 10 g (2 teaspoons) salt
- sunflower oil for brushing

KNEADING IN A STAND MIXER
Put the wheat bran, the 2 flours, water, starter, fresh yeast, and salt in the bowl. Knead with the dough hook for 4 minutes at low speed, then for 6 minutes at high speed.

KNEADING BY HAND
Put the bran and the 2 flours on a work surface or in a mixing bowl and make a large well in the center. Pour in half the water, then add the starter, the fresh yeast, and the salt. Mix well, then add the rest of the water and blend until all the flour has been incorporated. Knead the dough until it becomes smooth and elastic.

Shape the dough into a ball and cover with a damp cloth. Leave to rise for 45 minutes, by which time it will have increased in volume.

Dust the work surface. Gently reshape the dough into a ball, cover with a damp cloth, and leave it to rest for 30 minutes.

Brush the work surface with sunflower oil. Turn the balls over so the seams are on top, bring the edges to the center and press them down gently. Turn the dough over again and roll on the work surface, pressing gently, to form smooth, even-shaped balls. The oil will prevent the seam from reopening. Cover the dough with a damp cloth and leave to proof for 1 hour 30 minutes.

Place a baking sheet on the bottom shelf of the oven and preheat to 450°F (230°C). Turn out the dough onto another baking sheet lined with parchment [baking] paper, with the seam uppermost. Just before putting the loaf in the oven, pour 50 g (scant ¼ cup) of water onto the preheated baking sheet. Bake for 20–25 minutes.

Remove from the oven and leave to cool on a wire rack.

Specialty Breads

RYE BREAD

Makes 3 loaves,
each about 320 g

TIMINGS
- Mixing & kneading: 8 min
- First rising: 1 h
- Resting: 15 min
- Proofing: 1 h
- Baking: 30 min

INGREDIENTS
- 350 g (3½ cups) medium or dark rye flour
- 150 g (1¼ cups) all-purpose (plain) flour
- 360 g (scant 1½ cups) water at 68°F (20°C)
- 100 g (scant ½ cup) liquid sourdough starter (or 25 g [2 tablespoons] dry sourdough starter)
- 2 g (½ teaspoon) fresh baker's yeast
- 10 g (2 teaspoons) salt

KNEADING IN A STAND MIXER
Place all the ingredients in the bowl and knead with the dough hook for 7 minutes at low speed, then for 1 minute at high speed [1].

KNEADING BY HAND
Put the 2 flours on a work surface or in a mixing bowl and make a large well in the center. Pour in half the water, then add the starter, fresh yeast, and salt. Mix well, then add the rest of the water and blend until all the flour has been incorporated. Knead until the dough becomes smooth and elastic.

Shape into a ball and cover with a damp cloth. Leave to rise for 1 hour. By the end of the rising time, the dough will have increased in volume and little bubbles will form on the surface.

Dust the work surface. Divide the dough into 3 equal pieces [2], and shape them into balls. Cover with a damp cloth and leave to rest for 15 minutes.

Working with 1 piece of dough at a time, use the palm of your hand to flatten it gently into a rough oval. With the long side facing you, fold in a third towards the center [3] and press along the edge with your fingertips. Swivel the dough 180 degrees. Fold in the other long edge so that it overlaps in the center and press with the heel of your hand [4]. Fold one half on top of the other, and seal the edges together with the heel of your hand [5]. With lightly floured hands, roll the dough out to form an oval [6]. Shape the other 2 loaves the same way.

Place the loaves, seams underneath, on a floured baker's cloth, making folds to separate them (or you could place the loaves directly onto a baking sheet lined with parchment [baking] paper). Lightly dust the loaves with rye flour [7]. Score them in a chevron pattern (page 41), leaving a finger's width between the 2 rows of slashes [8]. Leave to proof for 1 hour, by which time little bubbles will appear on the surface of the loaves and the incisions will have stretched and widened.

Place a baking sheet on the bottom shelf of the oven and preheat to 430°F (225°C). Gently lift the loaves onto another baking sheet lined with parchment (baking) paper. Just before putting them in the oven, pour 50 g (scant ¼ cup) of water onto the preheated baking sheet. Bake the loaves for 30 minutes.

Remove from the oven and leave to cool on a wire rack.

△ Do not let the proofing last too long, otherwise the dough may collapse.

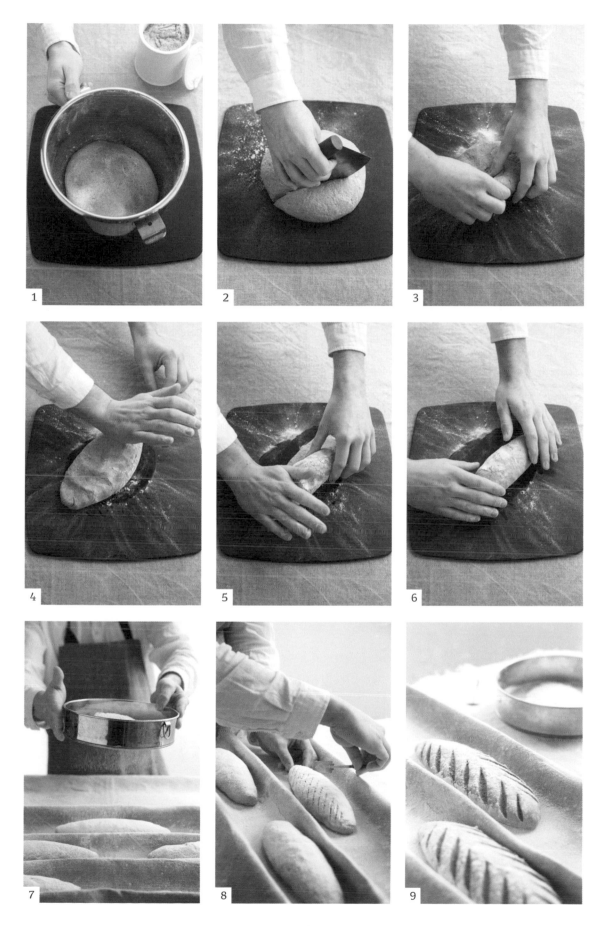

MASLIN LOAF

Makes 1 loaf, about 960 g

TIMINGS
- Mixing & kneading: 9 min
- First rising: 1 h 30 min
- Resting: 15 min
- Proofing: 1 h 30 min
- Baking: 25 min

INGREDIENTS
- 250 g (2½ cups) medium or dark rye flour, plus extra for dusting
- 250 g (2 cups) all-purpose (plain) flour
- 350 g (1½ cups) water at 68°F (20°C)
- 100 g (scant ½ cup) liquid sourdough starter (or 25 g [2 tablespoons] dry sourdough starter)
- 2 g (½ teaspoon) fresh baker's yeast, crumbled
- 10 g (2 teaspoons) salt

KNEADING IN A STAND MIXER
Place all the ingredients in the bowl and knead with the dough hook for 7 minutes at low speed, then for 2 minutes at high speed.

KNEADING BY HAND
Put the 2 flours on a work surface or in a mixing bowl and make a large well in the center. Pour in half the water, then add the starter, fresh yeast, and salt. Mix well, then add the rest of the water and blend until all the flour has been incorporated. Knead the dough until it becomes smooth and elastic.

Shape the dough into a ball. Cover with a damp cloth and leave to rise for 1 hour 30 minutes. The dough will have increased in volume by the end of the rising time.

Dust the work surface. Turn out the dough and carefully shape it into a ball. Leave to rest for 15 minutes under a damp cloth.

Place the dough on a lightly floured work surface and flatten it gently [1]. Turn it over then bring the edges in towards the center [2, 3, 4]. With your fingers pressed into the center of the dough [5], roll it over on itself and turn the seam to the underside [6]. Turn the dough around in your hands to form a smooth, even-shaped ball [7].

Place the dough on a board or directly onto a baking sheet lined with parchment (baking) paper, seam underneath. Cover with a damp cloth and leave to proof for 1 hour 30 minutes.

Place a baking sheet on the bottom shelf of the oven and preheat to 450°F (230°C). Dust the loaf with rye flour [8]. Score a cross on top [9]. Just before putting the loaf in the oven, pour 50 g (scant ¼ cup) of water onto the preheated baking sheet. Bake for 10 minutes, then lower the temperature to 410°F (210°C) and bake for another 15 minutes.

Remove from the oven and leave to cool on a wire rack.

△ The word *méteil* comes from the Latin *mistilium* (`mixed`), which derives from the classical Latin *mixtus*. The term designates a mixture of various cereals, or of cereals and legumes which, in medieval times, were sown and harvested together. In baking, *méteil* is used to mean a mixture of equal parts rye and wheat, although nowadays the 2 cereals are rarely cultivated together. The English version of *pain de méteil* is `maslin.`

Specialty Breads

Maslin Loaf

Specialty Breads

GLUTEN-FREE CORN BREAD

Makes 6 small loaves,
each about 140 g

TIMINGS
- Preparation: 30 min
- Baking: 25 min

INGREDIENTS
- 220 g (scant 1 cup) milk
- 330 g (2 cups) fine cornmeal
- 7 g salt (1 heaping teaspoon)
- 60 g (¼ cup) butter, plus extra for greasing
- 80 g egg yolks
- 20 g (2 tablespoons) fresh baker's yeast, crumbled
- 120 g egg whites

Put two-thirds of the milk, cornmeal, salt, and butter in a saucepan [1]. Cook over low heat for 10 minutes, whisking briskly all the time, until the mixture takes on the consistency of polenta [2]. Leave to cool.

Whisk the egg yolks in a large bowl until creamy [3]. Put the rest of the milk and the fresh yeast into another mixing bowl [4] and whisk to blend well.

Pour the egg yolks into the yeast mixture [5] and whisk until the mixture becomes smooth and creamy [6]. Gradually incorporate the cornmeal mixture, little by little, and whisk until it becomes a smooth dough, scraping down the sides of the bowl regularly with a spatula [7, 8].

Whisk the egg whites to fluffy peaks [9]. Fold around a fifth of the mixture into the dough, then carefully incorporate the remainder, using a spatula [10].

Place a baking sheet on the bottom shelf of the oven and preheat to 450°F (230°C). Brush six 4-inch (10-cm) mini-loaf pans with melted butter. Fill each pan two-thirds full of dough and smooth the top [11]. Just before putting the loaves in the oven, pour 50 g (scant ¼ cup) of water onto the preheated baking sheet. Bake for 25 minutes.

Turn out the loaves and leave to cool on a wire rack.

Specialty Breads

GLUTEN-FREE CHESTNUT FLOUR BREAD

Makes 1 loaf, about 910 g

TIMINGS
- Preparation: 25 min
- Resting: 1 h
- Baking: 25 min
  + 10 min standing

INGREDIENTS
- 5 g (1½ teaspoons) fresh baker's yeast, crumbled
- 400 g (scant 4½ cups) chestnut flour
- 100 g (scant 1 cup) soy flour
- 400 g (1⅔ cups) water at 68°F (20°C)
- 10 g (2 teaspoons) salt

As it doesn't contain gluten, chestnut flour cannot rise without the addition of fresh baker's yeast. Begin by measuring this out [1].

KNEADING IN A STAND MIXER
Put the 2 flours, water, fresh yeast, and salt in the bowl. Knead with the dough hook at low speed until it becomes a rather coarse, crumbly dough.

KNEADING BY HAND
Put the 2 flours in a mixing bowl and make a large well in the center. Pour in half the water and the fresh yeast [2]. Mix well, then gradually add the rest of the water and the salt [3], and continue to mix until all the flour has been incorporated [4].

Dust a banneton with soy flour [5] and put in the dough, which should fill it by two-thirds. Dust with chestnut flour and leave to rest for 1 hour [6].

Place a baking sheet on the bottom shelf of the oven and preheat to 450°F (230°C). Carefully turn out the banneton onto another baking sheet lined with parchment (baking) paper. Just before putting the loaf in the oven, pour 50 g (scant ¼ cup) of water onto the preheated baking sheet. Bake for 25 minutes, then turn off the oven and leave the loaf in the oven for another 10 minutes.

Remove from the oven and leave to cool on a wire rack.

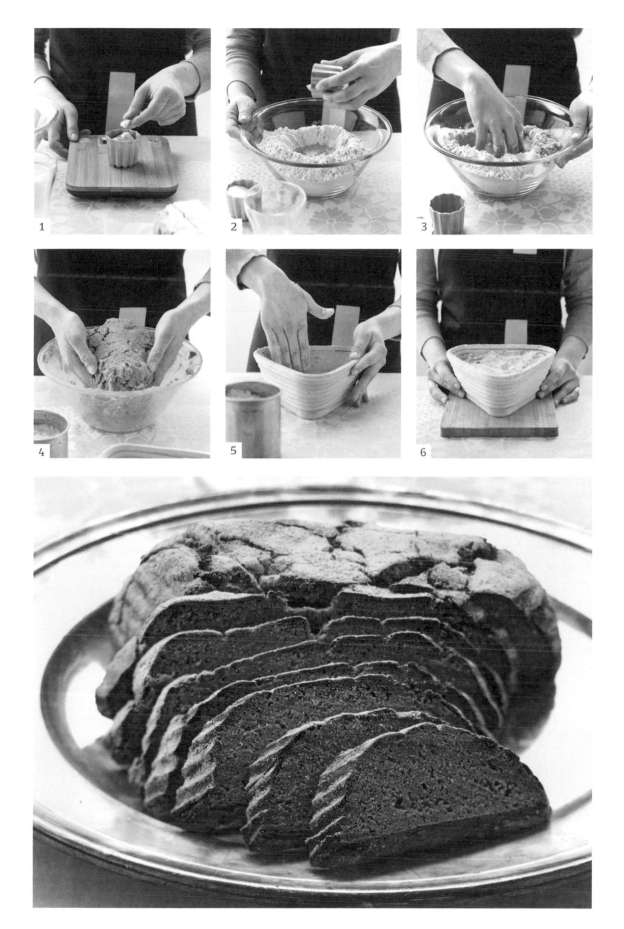

ROSEMARY FOCACCIA

Makes 1 large focaccia, about 940 g

TIMINGS

- Steeping the rosemary: 12 h
- Mixing & kneading: 15 min
- First rising: 2 h
- Proofing: 1 h 30 min
- Baking: 15-20 min

INGREDIENTS

- 4-5 sprigs fresh rosemary
- 30 g (2 tablespoons) extra-virgin olive oil, plus extra for drizzling
- 500 g (4 cups) all-purpose (plain) flour
- 330 g (1⅓ cup) water at 68°F (20°C)
- 100 g (scant ½ cup) liquid sourdough starter (or 25 g [2 tablespoons] dry sourdough starter)
- 7 g (2½ teaspoons) fresh baker's yeast
- 10 g (2 teaspoons) salt
- Sea salt flakes for sprinkling

The night before, remove the leaves from the fresh rosemary sprigs and mix them with the olive oil [1]. Leave to steep overnight at room temperature.

KNEADING IN A STAND MIXER

Put the flour, water, starter, yeast, and salt in the bowl. Knead with the dough hook for 5 minutes at low speed, then for 10 minutes at high speed. Add the rosemary and the steeping oil around 3 minutes before the end of the kneading time.

KNEADING BY HAND

Put the flour on a work surface or in a mixing bowl and make a large well in the center. Pour in half the water, then add the starter, fresh yeast, and salt. Mix well, then add the rest of the water and knead until all the flour has been incorporated. Add the rosemary and the steeping oil. Knead the dough until it becomes smooth and elastic [2].

Shape the dough into a ball, cover with a damp cloth, and leave to rise for 2 hours. Midway through the rise, deflate the dough by folding it in half. By the end of the rising time it will have increased in volume.

Put the dough in a shallow baking pan lined with parchment (baking) paper. Stretch the dough with your hands to make a flat piece that fills a 16 × 12-inch (40 × 30-cm) pan. Cover with a damp cloth and leave to proof for 1 hour 30 minutes.

Place a baking sheet on the bottom shelf of the oven and preheat to 450°F (230°C). Use the tips of your fingers to press small holes over the surface of the focaccia [3]. Pour a little oil into the holes [4] and sprinkle with salt flakes. Just before putting the focaccia in the oven, pour 50 g (scant ¼ cup) of water onto the preheated baking sheet. Bake for 15-20 minutes.

Remove from the oven, turn out the focaccia, and leave to cool on a wire rack.

Specialty Breads

Rosemary Focaccia

Specialty Breads

MACATIA BREAD

Makes 2 loaves,
each about 490 g

TIMINGS
- Mixing & kneading: 10 min
- First rising: 2 h
- Resting: 30 min
- Proofing: 2 h
- Baking: 12-13 min

INGREDIENTS
- 500 g (4 cups)
  all-purpose (plain) flour,
  pus extra for dusting
- 250 g water at 68°F (20°C)
- 100 g (scant ½ cup)
  liquid sourdough starter
  (or 25 g [2 tablespoons]
  dry sourdough starter)
- 10 g (1 tablespoon)
  fresh baker's yeast
- 10 g (2 teaspoons) salt
- 125 g (½ cup)
  demerara sugar
- 10 g (2½ teaspoons)
  vanilla extract or seeds
  from 1 vanilla bean
- Peanut oil for greasing

KNEADING IN A STAND MIXER
Put the flour, water, starter, fresh yeast, salt, and sugar in the bowl. Knead with the dough hook for 10 minutes at high speed. Add the vanilla around 2 minutes before the end of the kneading time.

KNEADING BY HAND
Put the flour on a work surface or in a mixing bowl and make a large well in the center. Pour in half the water, the starter, the fresh yeast, salt, and sugar. Mix well, then add the remaining water and the vanilla and mix until all the flour is incorporated. Knead the dough until it becomes smooth and elastic.

Shape the dough into a ball, cover with a damp cloth, and leave to rise for 2 hours. The dough will have increased in volume by the end of the rising time.

Dust the work surface. Divide the dough into 2 equal pieces. Cover with a damp cloth and leave to rest for 30 minutes.

Oil another part of the work surface with peanut oil [1]. Roll the dough between your hands and on the work surface, pressing gently, to form smooth, even-shaped balls with a defined oval seam [2, 3, 4]. The oil prevents the seams from closing up as the dough expands during the baking.

Move the dough balls to the floured work surface, seams underneath [5]. Cover with a damp cloth and leave to proof for 2 hours. They will have increased in volume by the end of the rising time [6].

Place a baking sheet on the bottom shelf of the oven and preheat to 410°F (210°C). Turn the dough over onto a wire rack or baking sheet lined with parchment (baking) paper, seams on top. Just before putting the loaves in the oven, pour 50 g (scant ¼ cup) of water onto the preheated baking sheet. Bake for 12-13 minutes.

Remove from the oven and leave to cool on a wire rack.

△ The invention of Macatia bread dates back to the slavery era on Réunion, formerly known as the Bourbon Isle. It was an active center of slavery until its abolishment in 1848. The word "macatia" is said to derive from the East African Swahili word for bread, *mkate*. I was taught how to make this bread by my friend Norbert Tacoun, the great Réunion baker.

Specialty Breads

EKMEK

Makes 3 loaves, each about 310 g

TIMINGS
- Mixing & kneading: 10 min
- First rising: 1h
- Resting: 15 min
- Proofing: 2h
- Baking: 20 min

INGREDIENTS
- 500 g (4 cups) all-purpose (plain) flour, plus extra for dusting
- 225 g (scant 1 cup) water at 68°F (20°C)
- 100 g (scant ½ cup) liquid sourdough starter (or 25 g [2 tablespoons] dry sourdough starter)
- 5 g (1¾ teaspoons) fresh baker's yeast
- 10 g (2 teaspoons) salt
- 75 g (⅓ cup) clear honey
- 40 g (scant ¼ cup) extra-virgin olive oil

KNEADING IN A STAND MIXER
Put the flour, water, starter, fresh yeast, salt, and honey in the bowl. Knead with the dough hook for 5 minutes at low speed, then for 2 minutes at high speed. Add the oil and continue to knead for another 3 minutes.

KNEADING BY HAND
Put the flour on a work surface or in a mixing bowl and make a large well in the center. Pour in half the water, starter, fresh yeast, salt, and honey. Mix well, then add the rest of the water and then the oil. Mix until all the flour is incorporated. Knead the dough until it becomes smooth and elastic.

Shape the dough into a ball, then cover with a damp cloth and leave to rise for 1 hour. The dough will have increased in volume by the end of the rising time.

Dust the work surface. Divide the dough into 3 equal pieces. Working with 1 ball at a time, bring the edges to the center. Turn the dough over and roll on the work surface, pressing gently, to form a smooth, even-shaped ball. Shape the other pieces of dough in the same way. Cover with a damp cloth, seams underneath, and leave to rest for 15 minutes.

Use the palm of your hand to flatten each piece of dough [1, 2]. Place them on a baking sheet lined with parchment (baking) paper. Cover with a damp cloth and leave to proof for 2 hours.

Place a baking sheet on the bottom shelf of the oven and preheat to 450°F (230°C). Score the loaves in a crosshatch pattern [3]. Just before putting them in the oven, pour 50 g (scant ¼ cup) of water onto the preheated baking sheet. Bake for 20 minutes.

Remove from the oven and leave to cool on a wire rack.

△ EKMEK WITH DRIED RASPBERRIES
   Add 190 g (1⅔ cups) dried raspberries (20% of the dough's total weight) toward the end of the kneading process. Score in a swirl pattern (see page 39) before baking.

△ EKMEK WITH BLACK SESAME SEEDS
   Spread black sesame seeds on a plate. After flattening the dough, brush or spray with a little water and press into the seeds. Score with a cross (see page 38) before baking.

Specialty Breads

PUMPER-NICKEL

Makes 2 loaves,
each about 615 g

TIMINGS
- Mixing & kneading: 8 min
- First rising: 1 h
- Proofing: 16–20 h
- Baking: 6 h

INGREDIENTS
- 300 g (2 cups) dark rye flour
- 150 g (1 1/4 cup)
  all-purpose (plain) flour
- 50 g (generous 1/4 cup)
  precooked bulgur wheat
- 500 g (generous 2 cups)
  water at 80°F (25°C)
- 120 g liquid sourdough
  starter (or 25 g [2
  tablespoons] dry
  sourdough starter)
- 10 g (2 teaspoons) salt
- 60 g (1/4 cup) clear honey
- 40 g (1/4 cup) mixed seeds
  (anise, coriander, fennel,
  and caraway)
- Butter for greasing

You will need 2 loaf pans with sliding lids, each 6 1/2 × 3 × 3 inches (17 × 7.5 × 7.5 cm). Alternatively, use ordinary loaf pans, although you won't get the same oblong shape.

KNEADING IN A STAND MIXER
Put the 2 flours, bulgur wheat, water, starter, salt, and honey in the bowl. Knead with the dough hook for 4 minutes at low speed, then for 4 minutes at high speed. Add the mixed seeds towards the end of the kneading time [1], and knead until the mixture is creamy [2].

KNEADING BY HAND
Put the 2 flours and the bulgur wheat in a mixing bowl and make a large well in the center. Pour in half the water, starter, salt, and honey. Mix well, then add the remaining water and knead until all the flour is incorporated. Add the mixed seeds and knead until the mixture is creamy.

Cover the bowl with a damp cloth and leave the dough to rest for 1 hour [3]. It will have increased in volume by the end of the rising time.

Butter the loaf pans and their lids. Fill them two-thirds full with the dough and smooth the surface [4]. Close the lids [5] and leave to proof for 16–20 hours, by which time the dough will have expanded to almost fill the pans.

Preheat the oven to 230°F (110°C). Make sure the lids are on securely and bake for 6 hours.

Remove from the oven, turn out the loaves, and leave to cool on a wire rack.

△ The deep chocolate-brown color of pumpernickel is not due to any added ingredient but to the rye flour, from which it is almost exclusively made, and from the time it spends inside the oven. The long fermentation and baking times give it a unique flavor.

Pumpernickel   134

Specialty Breads

BROA

Makes 3 loaves,
each about 320 g

TIMINGS
- Mixing & kneading: 9 min
- First rising: 1 h
- Resting: 30 min
- Proofing: 1 h 10 min
- Baking: 25 min

INGREDIENTS
- 250 g (1½ cups) fine cornmeal
- 250 g (2 cups) all-purpose (plain) flour
- 330 g (1⅓ cups) water at 68°F (20°C)
- 100 g (scant ½ cup) liquid sourdough starter (or 25 g [2 tablespoons] dry sourdough starter)
- 5 g (1½ teaspoons) fresh baker's yeast
- 10 g (2 teaspoons) salt
- 30 g (2 tablespoons) canola (rapeseed) oil

KNEADING IN A STAND MIXER
Put the cornmeal, flour, water, starter, fresh yeast, and salt in the bowl. Knead with the dough hook for 4 minutes at low speed, then for 3 minutes at high speed. Add the canola (rapeseed) oil and knead for another 2 minutes.

KNEADING BY HAND
Put the cornmeal and flour on the work surface or in a mixing bowl and make a large well in the center. Pour in half the water, then add the starter, fresh yeast, and salt. Mix well, then add the remaining water and mix until all the flour is incorporated. Knead the dough until it becomes smooth and elastic. Add the canola (rapeseed) oil towards the end of the kneading time.

Shape the dough into a ball, then cover with a damp cloth and leave to rise for 1 hour. The dough will have increased in volume by the end of the rising time.

Dust the work surface. Divide the dough into 3 equal pieces. Shape into balls without working the dough too much. Cover with a damp cloth and leave to rest for 30 minutes.

Turn the balls over on the work surface. Bring the edges to the center and press them down gently. Turn so the seams are underneath and roll on the work surface, pressing gently, to form smooth, even-shaped balls. Shape the other loaves the same way.

Put the loaves in floured banneton baskets, seams underneath. Cover with a damp cloth and leave to proof for 1 hour 10 minutes.

Place a baking sheet on the bottom shelf of the oven and preheat to 410°F (210°C). Carefully turn out the loaves, seams on top, onto another baking sheet lined with parchment (baking) paper. Don't score them. Just before putting the loaves in the oven, pour 50 g (scant ¼ cup) of water onto the preheated baking sheet. Bake for 25 minutes.

Remove from the oven and leave to cool on a wire rack.

△ *Broa* is to Portugal what farmhouse bread is to France, with a yellow crumb and a crunchy crust.

Specialty Breads

BAGELS

Makes 9 bagels,
each about 100 g

TIMINGS

- Mixing & kneading: 10 min
- First rising: 1 h
- Resting time: 15 min
- Proofing: 30 min
- Boiling: 30 min
- Baking: 15 min

INGREDIENTS

- 500 g (4 cups) all-purpose
  (plain) flour, plus extra
  for dusting
- 200 g (scant 1 cup)
  water at 68°F (20°C)
- 100 g (scant ½ cup)
  liquid sourdough starter
  (or 25 g [2 tablespoons]
  dry sourdough starter)
- 5 g (1½ teaspoons)
  fresh baker's yeast
- 10 g (2 teaspoons) salt
- 20 g (2 tablespoons) sugar
- 2 eggs
- 25 g (2 tablespoons)
  softened butter
- Poppy and sesame seeds
  for topping

KNEADING IN A STAND MIXER

Put the flour, water, starter, fresh yeast, salt, sugar, and egg in the mixing bowl. Knead with the dough hook for 4 minutes at low speed, then for 3 minutes at high speed. Add the butter and knead at high speed for another 3 minutes.

KNEADING BY HAND

Put the flour on a work surface or in a mixing bowl and make a large well in the center. Pour in half the water, then add the starter, fresh yeast, salt, sugar, and egg. Mix well, then add the remaining water and knead until all the flour is incorporated. Add the butter and knead the dough until it becomes smooth and elastic.

Put the dough onto a floured work surface [1]. Use your hands to flatten and roll it into a rough oblong [2, 3]. Use a dough cutter to divide the dough into 9 equal piece [4]. Cover with a damp cloth and leave to rest for 15 minutes.

Roll each piece of dough under your hands to form nicely rounded balls [5, 6]. Dust the tops with flour, then push your finger into the center of each ball to form a hole [7]. Gradually stretch the holes and widen them to a diameter of around 1 inch (2.5 cm) to create the traditional bagel ring [8, 9, 10]. Cover the bagels with a damp cloth and leave to proof for 30 minutes.

Bring a large saucepan of water to a boil. Reduce to a simmer, then lower in the bagels, 1 at a time, with a slotted spoon [11]. Cook for 1 minute 30 seconds, then turn the bagels over in the simmering water and cook for another 1 minute 30 seconds. They will expand as they cook [12]. Let the bagels drain on a wire rack set above the sink. Cook the remaining bagels the same way.

Prepare 2 large plates, 1 covered with poppy seeds, the other with sesame seeds. In a small bowl, lightly beat the egg. Brush the cooked bagels lightly with beaten egg, then roll them in poppy or sesame seeds. Leave some plain. Arrange them on baking sheets lined with parchment (baking) paper.

Place another baking sheet on the bottom shelf of the oven and preheat to 400°F (200°C). Just before putting the bagels in the oven, pour 50 g (scant ¼ cup) of water onto the preheated baking sheet. Bake for 15 minutes.

Remove from the oven and leave to cool on a wire rack.

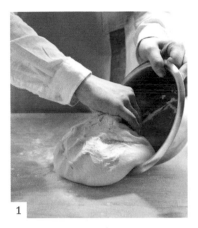

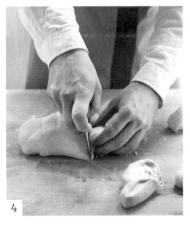

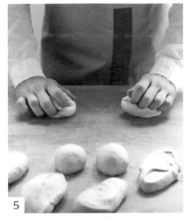

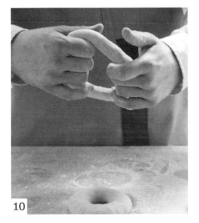

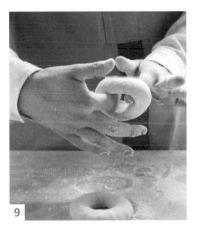

139

SESAME BUNS

Makes 10 buns, each about 100 g

TIMINGS
- Mixing & kneading: 15 min
- First rising: 1 h
- Resting time: 15 min
- Proofing: 2 h
- Baking: 14 min

INGREDIENTS
- 500 g (4 cups) all-purpose (plain) flour
- 200 g (scant 1 cup) water at 68°F (20°C)
- 100 g (scant ½ cup) liquid sourdough starter (or 20 g [2½ tablespoons] dry sourdough starter)
- 75 g egg yolks
- 16 g (5⅓ teaspoons) fresh baker's yeast
- 8 g (1½ teaspoons) salt
- 25 g (¼ cup) milk powder
- 35 g (scant ¼ cup) sugar
- 50 g (scant ¼ cup) softened butter
- 50 g (scant ¼ cup) sunflower oil, plus extra for brushing
- 10 g (1 tablespoon) cuttlefish or squid ink
- Sesame seeds for topping

You will need 2 silicone muffin pans (with 4½-inch [12-cm] diameter holes).

KNEADING IN A STAND MIXER
Put the flour, water, starter, egg yolks, fresh yeast, salt, milk powder, and sugar in the bowl. Knead with the dough hook for 5 minutes at low speed, then for 7 minutes at high speed. Add the butter and oil and knead for another 3 minutes [1]. Add the cuttlefish ink and mix until evenly blended [2].

KNEADING BY HAND
Put the flour on a work surface or in a mixing bowl and make a large well in the center. Pour in half the water, then add the starter, egg yolks, fresh yeast, salt, milk powder, and sugar. Mix well, then add the remaining water and mix until all the flour is incorporated. Add the softened butter, the oil, and the cuttlefish ink. Knead until well blended and the dough becomes smooth and elastic.

Shape the dough into a ball, then cover with a damp cloth. Leave to rise for 1 hour. The dough will have increased in volume by the end of the rising time.

Dust the work surface. Divide the dough into 10 equal pieces. Roll each piece of dough under your hands to form nicely rounded balls [3, 4]. Cover with a damp cloth and leave to rest for 15 minutes.

Spread a plate with sesame seeds. Brush the dough balls with oil. Dip them in the sesame seeds, to coat the tops [5], then put them in the muffin pans or arrange them on baking sheets lined with parchment (baking) paper. Cover with a damp cloth and leave to proof for 2 hours [6].

Place a baking sheet on the bottom shelf of the oven and preheat to 325°F (170°C). Just before putting the buns in the oven, pour 50 g (scant ¼ cup) of water onto the preheated baking sheet. Bake for 14 minutes.

Remove the buns from the oven, turn them out, and leave to cool on a wire rack.

143   Specialty Breads

SWISS "CROSS" BREAD

Makes 2 loaves,
each about 460 g

TIMINGS
- Mixing & kneading: 11min
- First rising: 2h
- Resting time: 30min
- Proofing: 1h 30min
- Baking: 25min

INGREDIENTS
- 450 g (3¾ cups)
  all-purpose (plain) flour,
  plus extra for dusting
- 50 g (½ cup) rye flour
- 320 g (generous 1¼ cup)
  water at 68°F (20°C)
- 100 g (scant ½ cup)
  liquid sourdough starter
  (or 25 g [2 tablespoons]
  dry sourdough starter)
- 5 g (1½ teaspoons)
  fresh baker's yeast
- 10 g (2 teaspoons) salt

KNEADING IN A STAND MIXER
Put the 2 flours, water, starter, yeast, and salt in the bowl. Knead with the dough hook for 4 minutes at low speed, then for 7 minutes at high speed.

KNEADING BY HAND
Put the 2 flours on the work surface or in a mixing bowl and make a large well in the center. Pour in half the water, then add the starter, the fresh yeast, and the salt. Mix well, then add the remaining water and mix until all the flour has been incorporated. Knead the dough until it becomes smooth and elastic.

Shape the dough into a ball, cover with a damp cloth, and leave to rise for 2 hours. Midway through the rise, deflate the dough by folding it in half. By the end of the rising time it will have increased in volume.

Dust the work surface. Divide the dough evenly into 2 equal pieces and shape into balls. Cover with a damp cloth and leave to rest for 30 minutes.

With a dough cutter, slice away around a fifth from each portion of dough. Roll these small pieces into even balls; they will form the "top knots" of the loaves [1]. To shape the loaves, turn them so the seams are on top, then bring the edges to the center and press them down gently [2]. Fold each piece over on itself, tucking the seam underneath [3]. Roll on the work surface, pressing gently, to form smooth, even-shaped balls [4].

Dust with flour. Use a rolling pin to press across the middle of each loaf [5], then push the edges together [6]. Swivel the loaves 90 degrees and press with the rolling pin again [7]. Push the edges in to form a cross shape. Sit the smaller balls of dough on top of each loaf and press them in gently [8]. Squeeze the edges of the loaves gently [9]. Cover with a damp cloth and leave to proof for 1 hour 30 minutes.

Place a baking sheet on the bottom shelf of the oven and preheat to 350°F (230°C). Arrange the loaves on another baking sheet lined with parchment (baking) paper. Just before putting the loaves in the oven, pour 50 g (a scant ¼ cup) of water onto the preheated baking sheet. Bake for 10 minutes, then lower the temperature to 410°F (210°C) and continue baking for another 15 minutes.

Remove from the oven and leave to cool on a wire rack.

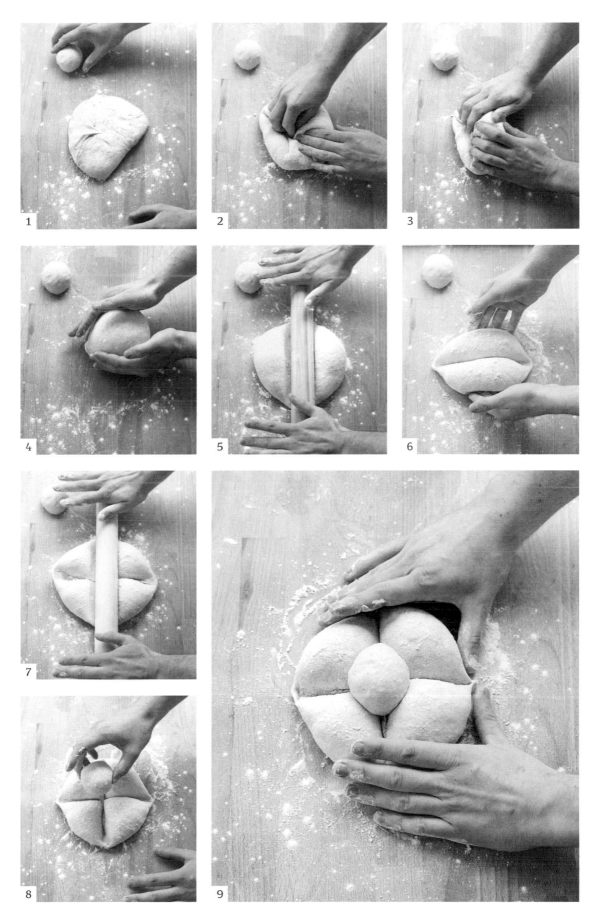

ORGANIC
NATURALLY-LEAVENED
BREADS

ORGANIC BAGUETTE

Makes 3 baguettes,
each about 310 g

TIMINGS

- Mixing & kneading: 16 min
- First resting: 1h
- First rising: 1h 15 min
- Second resting: 30 min
- Proofing: 1h 30 min
- Baking: 20 min

INGREDIENTS

- 500 g (4 cups) organic all-purpose (plain) flour
- 325 g (1⅓ cups) water at 68°F (20°C)
- 100 g (scant ½ cup) liquid sourdough starter (or 25 g [3 tablespoons] organic dry sourdough starter)
- 3 g (1 teaspoon) fresh baker's yeast, crumbled
- 10 g (2 teaspoons) salt

KNEADING IN A STAND MIXER

Put the flour and water in the bowl. Mix for 5 minutes at low speed. Remove the bowl from the machine and cover it with a slightly damp cloth. Leave to rest for 1 hour, then add the starter, the fresh yeast, and the salt. Knead with the dough hook for 4 minutes at low speed, then for 7 minutes at high speed.

KNEADING BY HAND

Put the flour on a work surface or in a mixing bowl and make a large well in the center. Pour in two-thirds of the water and mix until all the flour is incorporated. Leave to rest for 1 hour, covered with a damp cloth, then incorporate the rest of the water, the starter, fresh yeast, and salt. Knead the dough [1] until it becomes smooth and elastic.

Shape into a ball and cover with a damp cloth. Leave to rise for 1 hour 15 min. The dough will have increased in volume by the end of the rising time.

Dust the work surface. Divide the dough into 3 equal pieces. Fold each piece over on itself, pulling gently to stretch into a longish log. Leave to rest for 30 minutes, covered by a damp cloth.

Working with 1 piece of dough at a time, use the palm of your hand to flatten it gently. With the long side facing you, fold in a third towards the center and press along the edge with your fingertips. Swivel the dough 180 degrees. Fold in the other long edge so that it overlaps in the center and press again. Fold one half on top of the other and seal the edges together with the heel of your hand [2]. With lightly floured hands, roll the baguette out to 17 inches (45 cm) long [3], then pinch each end into a point. Shape the other 2 baguettes the same way.

Place the baguettes on a baking sheet lined with parchment (baking) paper, seams underneath. Cover with a damp cloth and leave to proof for 1 hour 30 minutes.

Place another baking sheet on the bottom shelf of the oven and preheat to 450°F (230°C). Lightly dust the baguettes with flour [4]. Score each one differently: make 6 crosshatch cuts on the first baguette, a single straight score on the second, and 3 oblique slashes on the third [5].

Just before putting the baguettes into the oven, pour 50 g (scant ¼ cup) of water onto the preheated baking sheet. Bake for around 20 minutes. Remove from the oven and leave to cool on a wire rack.

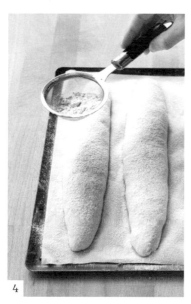

149   Organic Breads

SESAME
OR
POPPY-SEED
BAGUETTES

Prepare a large plate of sesame or poppy seeds (or scatter the seeds directly on the work surface).

Once the baguettes have been rolled out to the desired length, with the seams underneath, brush or spray them lightly with water.

Press the top of each baguette into the seeds, pushing down lightly to make them stick, then lift them onto a baking sheet lined with parchment (baking) paper, seams underneath. Cover with a damp cloth and leave to proof for 1 hour 30 minutes.

Score the loaves before putting them in the oven.

△ You could also use a mixture of seeds, such as flax, pumpkin, millet, and sunflower.

Organic Breads

ORGANIC STONE-GROUND BREAD

Makes 1 loaf, about 950 g

TIMINGS
- Mixing & kneading: 21min
- Resting: 2h
- First rising: 2h45min
- Proofing: 2h
- Baking: 40min

INGREDIENTS
- 150 g (1¼ cups) organic all-purpose (plain) flour, plus extra for dusting
- 350 g (scant 3 cups) organic fine stone-ground flour
- 320 g (generous 1¼ cups) water at 68°F (20°C)
- 125 g liquid sourdough starter (or 30 g organic dry sourdough starter)
- 1 g (⅓ teaspoon) fresh baker's yeast, crumbled
- 10 g (2 teaspoons) salt

KNEADING IN A STAND MIXER
Put the 2 flours and the water in the bowl. Mix for 6 minutes at low speed. Remove the bowl from the machine and cover it with a slightly damp cloth. Leave to rest for 2 hours, then add the starter, fresh yeast, and salt. Knead with the dough hook for 15 minutes at low speed.

KNEADING BY HAND
Place the 2 flours on a work surface or in a mixing bowl and make a large well in the center. Pour in two-thirds of the water. Mix until all the flour has been incorporated. Cover with a damp cloth and leave to rest for 2 hours. Mix in the rest of the water, the starter, the fresh yeast, and the salt. Knead the dough until it becomes smooth and elastic.

Shape into a ball and cover with a slightly damp cloth. Leave to rise for 2 hours 45 minutes. After 15 minutes, deflate the dough by folding it in half, and repeat 1 hour later. By the end of the rising time the dough will have increased in volume.

Place the dough on a lightly floured work surface. Turn it between your hands, pressing downwards. Put it in a well-floured banneton, seam on top. Bring the edges of the dough in towards the center and press them down gently to seal. Cover with a damp cloth and leave to proof for 2 hours.

Place a baking sheet on the bottom shelf of the oven and preheat to 450°F (230°C). Carefully turn out the banneton onto another baking sheet lined with parchment (baking) paper, seam underneath. Score a large square in the surface (see photo opposite).

Just before putting the loaf in the oven, pour 50 g (scant ¼ cup) of water onto the preheated baking sheet. Bake for 15 minutes, then lower the temperature to 400°F (200°C) and bake for another 25 minutes.

Remove from the oven and leave to cool on a wire rack.

Organic Breads

CLASSIC ORGANIC BREAD

Makes 2 loaves,
each about 460 g

TIMINGS
• Mixing & kneading: 8 min
• First rising: 2 h
• Resting: 30 min
• Proofing: 1 h 30 min
• Baking: 45 min

INGREDIENTS
• 500 g (4 cups) organic all-purpose flour
• 310 g (1¼ cups) water at 68°F (20°C)
• 100 g (scant ½ cup) liquid sourdough starter (or 25 g [3 tablespoons] organic dry sourdough starter)
• 1 g (⅓ teaspoon) fresh baker's yeast, crumbled
• 10 g (2 teaspoons) salt

KNEADING IN A STAND MIXER

Place all the ingredients in the bowl and knead with the dough hook for 4 minutes at low speed, then for another 4 minutes at high speed.

KNEADING BY HAND

Put the flour on a work surface or in a mixing bowl and make a large well in the center. Pour in half the water, then add the starter, fresh yeast, and salt. Mix well, then add the rest of the water and blend until all the flour has been incorporated. Knead the dough until it becomes smooth and elastic.

Shape the dough into a ball [1] and cover with a damp cloth. Leave to rise for 2 hours, by which time it will have increased in volume.

Dust the work surface. Divide the dough into 2 equal pieces [2]. Shape the dough between your hands, while pressing down on the work surface. Cover with a damp cloth and leave to rest for 30 minutes.

Reshape the balls of dough between your hands and place them on a baking sheet lined with parchment (baking) paper, seams underneath. Cover with a damp cloth and leave to proof for 1 hour 30 minutes. The dough will have increased in volume by the end of the proofing time [3].

Place another baking sheet on the bottom shelf of the oven and preheat to 450°F (230°C). Lightly dust the loaves with flour and score them in a swirl pattern [4] or with a cross (see pages 38–39).

Just before putting the loaves in the oven, pour 50 g (scant ¼ cup) of water onto the preheated baking sheet. Bake for 15 minutes, then lower the temperature to 400°F (200°C) and bake for another 30 minutes.

Remove from the oven and leave to cool on a wire rack.

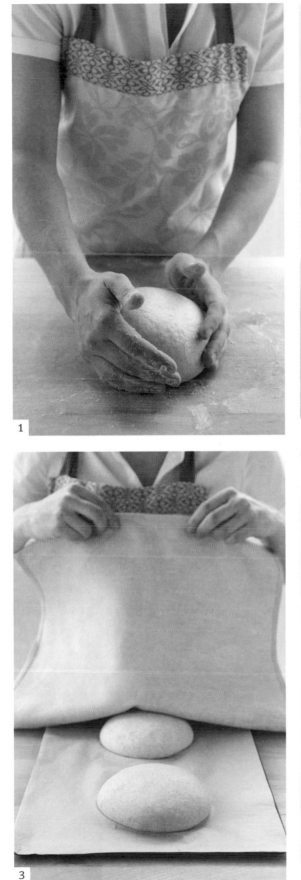

155

Classic Organic Bread   156

ORGANIC BUCK-WHEAT BREAD

Makes 2 loaves,
each about 450 g

TIMINGS
- Mixing & kneading: 10 min
- First rising: 2 h
- Proofing: 1 h 40 min
- Baking: 25–30 min

INGREDIENTS
- 300 g (2 1/2 cups) organic all-purpose (plain) flour, plus extra for dusting
- 200 g (1 1/2 cups) organic buckwheat flour
- 3 g (1/2 teaspoon) roasted malt (optional)
- 300 g (1 1/4 cups) water at 68°F (20°C)
- 100 g (scant 1/2 cup) liquid sourdough starter (or 25 g [3 tablespoons] organic dry sourdough starter)
- 1 g (1/3 teaspoon) fresh baker's yeast, crumbled
- 10 g (2 teaspoons) salt

KNEADING IN A STAND MIXER
Place all the ingredients in the bowl and knead with the dough hook for 4 minutes at low speed, then for 6 minutes at high speed.

KNEADING BY HAND
Place the 2 flours and the roasted malt, if using, on a work surface or in a mixing bowl and make a large well in the center. Pour in half the water, then add the starter, fresh yeast, and salt. Mix well, then add the rest of the water and blend until all the flour has been incorporated. Knead the dough until it becomes smooth and elastic.

Shape into a ball and cover with a damp cloth. Leave to rise for 2 hours. Midway through the rise, deflate the dough by folding it in half. By the end of the rising time, the dough will have increased in volume.

Dust the work surface. Flatten the dough gently without knocking out too much air. Shape into a rectangle about 16 × 8 inches (40 × 20 cm). Use a dough cutter to divide it lengthwise into 2 equal pieces.

Place the pieces of dough on a baking sheet lined with parchment (baking) paper. Cover with a damp cloth and leave to proof for 1 hour 40 minutes.

Place another baking sheet on the bottom shelf of the oven and preheat to 450°F (230°C). Dust the loaves with flour and score in a crosshatch pattern (see page 39), making 3 cuts in each direction. Just before putting the loaves in the oven, pour 50 g (scant 1/4 cup) of water onto the preheated baking sheet. Bake for 25–30 minutes.

Remove from the oven and leave to cool on a wire rack.

ORGANIC SPELT BREAD

Makes 3 loaves,
each about 320 g

TIMINGS
- Mixing & kneading: 8 min
- First rising: 1h 30 min
- Resting: 30 min
- Proofing: 1h 30 min
- Baking: 30 min

INGREDIENTS
- 325 g (2¾ cups) organic all-purpose (plain) flour, plus extra for dusting
- 175 g (1½ cups) organic spelt flour
- 310 g (1¼ cups) water at 68°F (20°C)
- 150 g (⅔ cup) liquid sourdough starter (or 30 g organic dry sourdough starter)
- 1 g (⅓ teaspoon) fresh baker's yeast, crumbled
- 10 g (2 teaspoons) salt

KNEADING IN A STAND MIXER
Put all the ingredients in the bowl. Knead with the dough hook for 4 minutes at low speed, then for another 4 minutes at high speed.

KNEADING BY HAND
Put the 2 flours on a work surface or in a mixing bowl and make a large well in the center. Pour in half the water, then add the starter, fresh yeast, and salt. Mix well, then add the rest of the water and blend until all the flour has been incorporated. Knead the dough until it becomes smooth and elastic.

Shape into a ball and cover with a damp cloth. Leave to rise for 1 hour 30 minutes. The dough will have increased in volume by the end of the rising time.

Dust the work surface. Divide the dough into 3 equal pieces and shape them into balls. Cover with a damp cloth and leave to rest for 30 minutes. Carefully flatten the dough pieces with the palm of your hand. If you wish, you can shape each piece differently.

TO MAKE A BATARD AND BAGUETTE
For the batard, fold in a third towards the center and press along the edge with your fingertips. Swivel the dough 180 degrees. Fold in the other long edge so that it overlaps in the center and press down again. Fold one half on top of the other, and seal the edges together with the heel of your hand. With lightly floured hands, roll into a plump oval. Repeat this process to make a baguette, then continue rolling to 20 inches (50 cm) long. Pinch the ends into a point. Place the loaves on a floured baker's cloth, seams upwards.

TO MAKE A BOULE
Place the dough on a lightly floured work surface. Turn it over, then bring the edges in towards the center and press down lightly [1, 2, 3]. Turn the dough over again, then use your hands to shape into an even ball [4]. Place on a floured baker's cloth, seam upwards.

Cover the 3 shaped loaves with a damp cloth and leave to proof for 1 hour 30 minutes. The dough will have increased in volume by the end of the proofing time.

Transfer the loaves, seams underneath, onto a baking sheet lined with parchment (baking) paper. Score the batard with 2 oblique slashes in 1 direction and 2 in the other; make 1 slash down the length of the baguette; score the boule in a crosshatch pattern (see pages 39–40).

Place another baking sheet on the bottom shelf of the oven and preheat to 450°F (230°C). Just before putting the loaves in the oven, pour 50 g (scant ¼ cup) of water onto the preheated baking sheet. Bake for around 30 minutes. Remove from the oven and leave to cool on a wire rack.

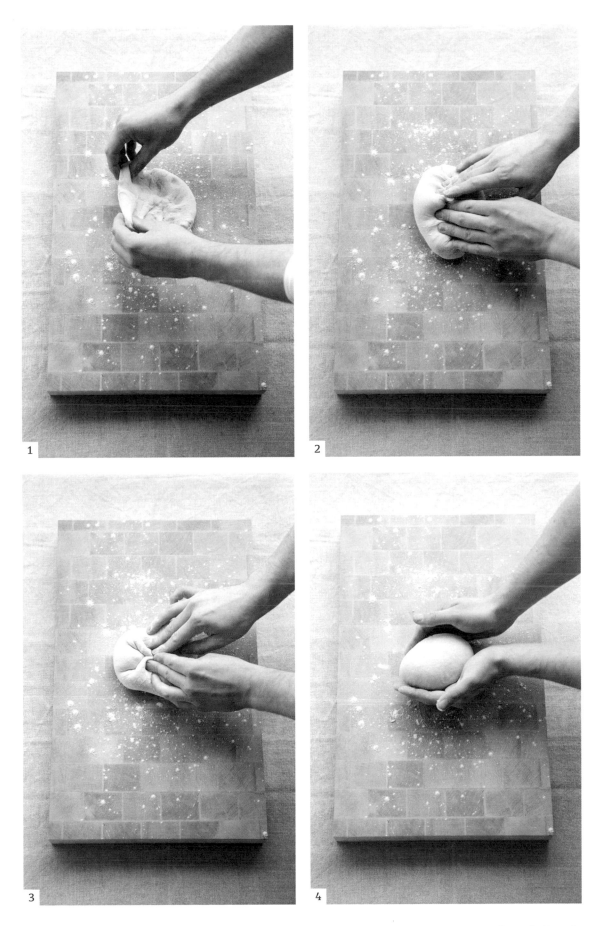

Organic Breads

Organic Spelt Bread   162

Organic Breads

ORGANIC EINKORN BREAD

Makes 1 loaf, about 890 g

TIMINGS
- Mixing & kneading: 8 min
- First rising: 1 h 30 min
- Proofing: 2 h
- Baking: 45 min

INGREDIENTS
- 450 g (3¾ cups) organic einkorn flour
- 50 g (scant ½ cup) organic all-purpose (plain) flour
- 310 g (1¼ cups) water at 68°F (20°C)
- 100 g (scant ½ cup) liquid sourdough starter (or 25 g [3 tablespoons] organic dry sourdough starter)
- 1 g (⅓ teaspoon) fresh baker's yeast, crumbled
- 10 g (2 teaspoons) salt

KNEADING IN A STAND MIXER
Place all the ingredients in the bowl. Knead with the dough hook for 4 minutes at low speed, then for another 4 minutes at high speed.

KNEADING BY HAND
Place the 2 flours on a work surface or in a mixing bowl and make a large well in the center. Pour in half the water, then add the starter, the fresh yeast, and the salt.
Mix well, then add the rest of the water and blend until all the flour has been incorporated. Knead the dough until it becomes smooth and elastic.

Place the dough on a lightly floured work surface. Fold it over upon itself once or twice [1]. Form into a round [2] and cover with a damp cloth. Leave to rise for 1 hour 30 minutes. The dough will have increased in volume by the end of the rising time [3].

Turn the dough around on the work surface. Bring the edges towards the center [4] and press lightly, then turn the dough over again to shape into a ball, tucking the seam underneath [5]. Put in a well-floured banneton, with the seam on top [6]. Cover with a damp cloth and leave to proof for 1 hour 30 minutes.

Place a baking sheet on the bottom shelf of the oven and preheat to 450°F (230°C). Carefully turn out the dough onto another baking sheet lined with parchment (baking) paper, seam underneath. Score the top in a cross shape.

Just before putting the loaf in the oven, pour 50 g (scant ¼ cup) of water onto the preheated baking sheet. Bake for 15 minutes, then lower the temperature to 410°F (210°C) and continue to bake for another 30 minutes.

Remove from the oven and leave to cool on a wire rack.

1

2

3

4

5

6

165 Organic Breads

ORGANIC WHOLE WHEAT BREAD

Makes 3 loaves,
each about 320 g

TIMINGS

• Mixing & kneading: 10 min
• First rising: 1h
• Resting: 15 min
• Proofing: 1h 30 min
• Baking: 25 min

INGREDIENTS

• 500 g (4 cups) organic
  coarse whole-wheat
  flour, plus extra for dusting
• 360 g (scant 1½ cups)
  water at 68°F (20°C)
• 100 g (⅓ cup) organic
  liquid sourdough starter
  (or 25 g [3 tablespoons]
  organic dry sourdough
  starter)
• 2 g (½ teaspoon) fresh
  baker's yeast, crumbled
• 10 g (2 teaspoons) salt
• sunflower oil for greasing

You will need 3 loaf pans with sliding lids, each ¾ × 8 × 3¼ inches (9.5 × 20 × 8 cm). Alternatively, use ordinary loaf pans, although you won't get the same square shape.

KNEADING IN A STAND MIXER

Place all the ingredients in the bowl and knead with the dough hook for 4 minutes at low speed, then for 6 minutes at high speed.

KNEADING BY HAND

Put the flour on a work surface or in a mixing bowl and make a large well in the center. Pour in half the water, then add the starter, fresh yeast, and salt. Mix well, then add the rest of the water and blend until all the flour has been incorporated [1]. Knead the dough by throwing it forcefully onto the work surface and folding it over on itself [2, 3], until it becomes smooth and elastic.

Shape into a ball and cover with a damp cloth. Leave to rise for 1 hour. The dough will have increased in volume by the end of the rising time.

Dust the work surface. Divide the dough into 3 equal pieces and shape them into balls. Cover with a damp cloth and leave to rest for 15 minutes.

Oil the 3 loaf pans and the inside of the lids. Working with 1 piece of dough at a time, use the palm of your hand to flatten it gently. With the long side facing you, fold in a third towards the center [4] and press along the edge with the heel of your hand. Swivel the dough 180 degrees. Turn the ends of the dough inwards to adjust the length so that it will fit the pan. Fold in a third, lengthwise, and press down again [5]. Fold one half on top of the other and seal the edges together with the heel of your hand. Shape the other 2 loaves the same way.

Place the loaves in the pans, seams underneath; they should take up between one-third and half the space. Close the lids and leave to rise for 1 hour 30 minutes, by which time the dough will have expanded to almost fill the pans [6].

Preheat the oven to 450°F (230°C). Make sure the lids are on securely, and then bake for 25 minutes.

Remove from the oven, turn out the loaves, and leave to cool on a wire rack.

1

2

3

4

5

6

Organic Breads

STONE-GROUND BREAD WITH CURRANT

Makes 1 loaf, about 1.1 kg

TIMINGS

- Mixing & kneading: 21 min
- Resting: 2 h
- First rising: 2 h 30 min
- Proofing: 2 h 30 min
- Baking: 40 min

INGREDIENTS

- 500 g (4 cups) organic stone-ground flour
- 320 g (generous 1 1/4 cups) water at 68°F (20°C)
- 125 g (1/2 cup) liquid sourdough starter (or 30 g [3 1/2 tablespoons] organic dry sourdough starter)
- 1 g (1/3 teaspoon) fresh baker's yeast, crumbled
- 10 g (2 teaspoons) salt
- 150 g (2/3 cup) currants

KNEADING IN A STAND MIXER

Put the flour and water in the bowl. Mix for 6 minutes. Remove the bowl from the machine and cover it with a damp cloth. Leave to rest for 2 hours, then add the starter, fresh yeast, and salt. Knead with the dough hook for 15 minutes at low speed. Add the currants and mix in well.

KNEADING BY HAND

Put the flour on a work surface or in a mixing bowl and make a large well in the center. Add two-thirds of the water and blend until all the flour has been incorporated. Leave to rest for 2 hours under a damp cloth, then mix in the rest of the water, the starter, the fresh yeast, and the salt. Mix well, then knead the dough until it becomes smooth and elastic. Add the currants at the end of the kneading.

Shape the dough into a ball and cover it with a damp cloth. Leave to rise for 2 hours 30 minutes. After 15 minutes, deflate the dough by folding it in half. Repeat an hour later. By the end of the rising time the dough will have increased in volume.

Dust the work surface. Roll the dough between your hands, pressing it gently into the work surface. Put it into a well-floured banneton, seam uppermost. Pick up the edges of the dough, bring them towards the center, and press down lightly to seal. Cover with a damp cloth and leave to proof for 2 hours 30 minutes.

Place a baking sheet on the bottom shelf of the oven and preheat to 450°F (230°C). Carefully turn out the loaf onto another baking sheet lined with parchment (baking) paper, seam underneath.

Score a large square on the surface (see page 39). Just before putting the loaves in the oven, pour 50 g (scant 1/4 cup) of water onto the preheated baking sheet. Bake for 15 minutes, then lower the temperature to 400°F (200°C) and bake for another 25 minutes.

Remove from the oven and leave to cool on a wire rack.

Organic Breads

BREADS
WITH
EXTRAS

HAZELNUT & BUTTER BREAD

Makes 4 loaves,
each about 290 g

TIMINGS
- Mixing & kneading: 15 min
- First rising: 1 h
- Resting: 15 min
- Proofing: 1 h 15 min
- Baking: 10 min + 20 min

INGREDIENTS
- 175 g (scant 1¼ cups) hazelnuts
- 500 g (4 cups) all-purpose (plain) flour, plus extra for dusting
- 250 g (1 cup) water at 68°F (20°C)
- 100 g (scant ½ cup) liquid sourdough starter (or 25 g [3 tablespoons] dry sourdough starter)
- 5 g (1½ teaspoons) fresh baker's yeast, crumbled
- 10 g (2 teaspoons) salt
- 25 g (¼ cup) milk powder
- 35 g (scant ¼ cup) sugar
- 75 g (⅓ cup) softened butter

Preheat the oven to 480°F (250°C). Spread the hazelnuts on a baking sheet lined with parchment (baking) paper and toast them for 10 minutes.

KNEADING IN A STAND MIXER
Put the flour, water, starter, fresh yeast, salt, milk powder, sugar, and butter in the bowl. Knead with the dough hook for 5 minutes at low speed, then for 10 minutes at high speed. Towards the end of the kneading time, add the hazelnuts and mix in at low speed.

KNEADING BY HAND
Put the flour on a work surface or in a mixing bowl and make a large well in the center. Pour in half the water, then add the starter, fresh yeast, salt, milk powder, and sugar. Mix well, then add the remaining water and blend until all the flour is incorporated. Mix in the butter, then knead the dough until it becomes smooth and elastic. Add the hazelnuts at the end of the kneading.

Shape into a ball and cover with a damp cloth. Leave to rise for 1 hour. Midway through the rise, deflate the dough by folding it in half. It will have increased in volume by the end of the rising time.

Dust the work surface. Divide the dough into 4 equal pieces and shape into balls. Cover with a damp cloth and leave to rest for 15 minutes.

Working with 1 piece of dough at a time, use the palm of your hand to flatten it gently into a rough oval. With the long side facing you, fold in a third towards the center and press along the edge with your fingertips. Swivel the dough 180 degrees. Fold in the other long edge so that it overlaps in the center and press again. Fold one half on top of the other and seal the edges together with the heel of your hand. With lightly floured hands, roll the dough out to form a plump oval. Shape the other 3 loaves the same way.

Place the loaves on a baking sheet lined with parchment (baking) paper, seams underneath. Score the top 7-8 times. Cover with a damp cloth and leave to proof for 1 hour 15 minutes.

Place another baking sheet on the bottom shelf of the oven and preheat to 450°F (230°C). Just before putting the loaves in the oven, pour 50 g (scant ¼ cup) of water onto the preheated baking sheet. Bake for 20 minutes.

Remove from the oven and leave to cool on a wire rack.

173   Breads with Extras

GORGON-ZOLA & WALNUT BREAD

Makes 4 loaves,
each about 280 g

TIMINGS

- Mixing & kneading: 15 min
- First rising: 1h 30 min
- Resting: 15 min
- Proofing: 1h
- Baking: 18 min

INGREDIENTS

- 500 g (4 cups) all-purpose (plain) flour, plus extra for dusting
- 325 g (1⅓ cups) water at 68°F (20°C)
- 100 g (scant ½ cup) liquid sourdough starter (or 25 g [3 tablespoons] dry sourdough starter)
- 5 g (1½ teaspoons) fresh baker's yeast, crumbled
- 10 g (2 teaspoons) salt
- 100 g (scant 1 cup) chopped walnuts (10% of the weight of the dough)
- 100 g gorgonzola (10% of the weight of the dough)

KNEADING IN A STAND MIXER

Put the flour, water, starter, fresh yeast, and salt in the bowl. Knead with the dough hook for 5 minutes at low speed, then for 10 minutes at high speed. Towards the end of the kneading time, add the walnuts and mix in at low speed.

KNEADING BY HAND

Put the flour on a work surface or in a mixing bowl and make a large well in the center. Pour in half the water, then add the starter, fresh yeast, and salt. Mix well, then add the rest of the water and mix until all the flour has been incorporated. Knead the dough until it becomes smooth and elastic. Add the walnuts at the end of the kneading time [1].

Shape the dough into a ball [2], and cover it with a damp cloth. Leave to rise for 1 hour 30 minutes. Midway through the rise, deflate the dough by folding it in half. By the end of the rising time it will have increased in volume.

Dust the work surface. Divide the dough into 4 equal pieces. Fold each piece over on itself, pulling gently to stretch into a longish log [3]. Cover with a damp cloth and leave to rest for 15 minutes.

Slice the gorgonzola into thin pieces. Working with 1 piece of dough at a time, use the palm of your hand to flatten it gently and top with a quarter of the cheese [4]. Fold a third of the dough in towards the center and press along the edge with your fingertips. Swivel the dough 180 degrees. Fold one half on top of the other and seal the edges together with the heel of your hand. With lightly floured hands, roll out to 9 inches (20 cm) [5]. Shape the other 3 loaves the same way.

Place the dough on a baking sheet lined with parchment (baking) paper, seams underneath. Cover with a damp cloth and leave to proof for 1 hour.

Preheat the oven to 480°F (250°C). Score each loaf along its length [6]. Brush or spray lightly with water and bake for 18 minutes.

Remove from the oven and leave to cool on a wire rack.

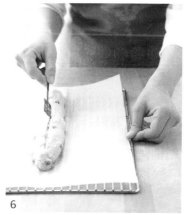

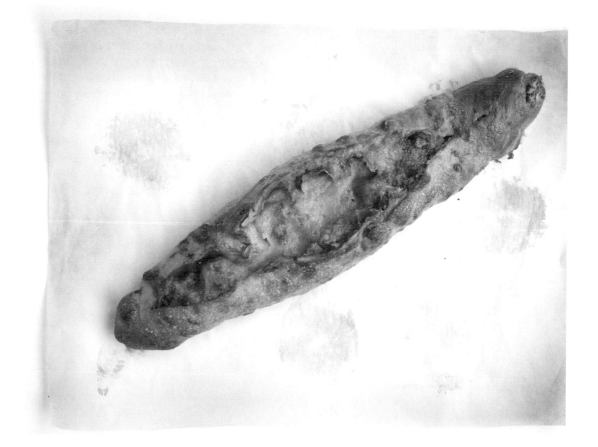

Breads with Extras

GREEN TEA & ORANGE LOAF

Makes 4 loaves,
each about 260 g

TIMINGS

- Mixing & kneading: 15 min
- First rising: 2 h
- Resting: 15 min
- Proofing: 1 h 15 min
- Baking: 18 min

INGREDIENTS

- 150 g (scant 1 cup)
  candied orange peel
- 500 g (4 cups) all-purpose
  (plain) flour, plus extra
  for dusting
- 250 g (1 cup) water
  at 68°F (20°C)
- 100 g (scant ½ cup)
  liquid sourdough starter
  (or 25 g [3 tablespoons]
  dry sourdough starter)
- 2 g (½ teaspoon) fresh
  baker's yeast, crumbled
- 10 g (2 teaspoons) salt
- 30 g (2 tablespoons)
  olive oil
- 25 g (5 teaspoons)
  orange-flower water
- 10 g (2 teaspoons) matcha
  green tea powder

Finely dice the orange peel [1].

KNEADING IN A STAND MIXER

Put the flour, water, starter, fresh yeast, and salt in the bowl. Knead with the dough hook for 5 minutes at low speed, then for 8 minutes at high speed. Mix in the oil and knead for another 2 minutes, then switch the machine off and add the orange-flower water and matcha green tea powder [2]. Continue kneading at low speed; the dough will turn green [3]. Add the diced orange peel and mix in at low speed.

KNEADING BY HAND

Put the flour on a work surface or in a mixing bowl and make a large well in the center. Pour in half the water, then add the starter, fresh yeast, and salt. Mix well, then add the rest of the water, the oil, and orange-flower water and blend until all the flour has been incorporated. Add the matcha green tea powder and orange peel and knead the dough until it becomes evenly colored, smooth, and elastic.

Shape into a ball and cover with a damp cloth. Leave to rise for 2 hours. Midway through the rise, deflate the dough by folding it in half. The dough will have increased in volume by the end of the rising time.

Dust the work surface. Divide the dough into 4 equal pieces and shape them into balls. Cover with a damp cloth and leave to rest for 15 minutes.

Roll each piece of dough between your hands, pressing gently into the work surface, until smooth and well-rounded.

Place the loaves on a baking sheet lined with parchment (baking) paper, seams underneath. Leave to proof for 1 hour 15 minutes, covered with a damp cloth.

Place another baking sheet on the bottom shelf of the oven and preheat to 450°F (230°C). Score the loaves in a crosshatch pattern (see page 39) [4]. Just before putting the loaves in the oven, pour 50 g (scant ¼ cup) of water onto the preheated baking sheet. Bake for 18 minutes.

Remove from the oven and leave to cool on a wire rack.

Breads with Extras

179

ORANGE BREAD

Makes 4 loaves,
each about 260 g

TIMINGS
- Mixing & kneading: 15 min
- First rising: 2 h
- Resting: 15 min
- Proofing: 1 h
- Baking: 30 min

INGREDIENTS
- 500 g (4 cups) all-purpose (plain) flour, plus extra for dusting
- 310 g (1¼ cups) water at 68°F (20°C)
- 100 g (scant ½ cup) liquid sourdough starter (or 25 g [3 tablespoons] dry sourdough starter)
- 5 g (1½ teaspoons) fresh baker's yeast, crumbled
- 40 g (scant ¼ cup) sugar
- 10 g (2 teaspoons) salt
- 25 g (1¾ tablespoons) softened butter, plus extra for greasing
- 25 g (5 teaspoons) orange-flower water
- 95 g (scant ⅔ cup) candied orange peel, cut into thin strips

You will need 3 loaf pans with sliding lids, each 3¼ × 3 × 3 inches (18 × 8.5 × 7.5 cm). Alternatively, use ordinary loaf pans, although you won't get the same square shape.

KNEADING IN A STAND MIXER
Put the flour, water, starter, fresh yeast, sugar, and salt in the bowl. Knead with the dough hook for 5 minutes at low speed, then for 8 minutes at high speed. Mix in the butter and knead for another 2 minutes. Mix in the orange-flower water briefly at low speed.

KNEADING BY HAND
Put the flour on a work surface or in a mixing bowl and make a large well in the center. Pour in half the water, then add the starter, fresh yeast, and salt. Mix, then add the rest of the water, the orange-flower water, and sugar. Blend until all the flour has been incorporated. Add the butter and knead the dough until it becomes smooth and elastic.

Shape into a ball and cover with a damp cloth. Leave to rise for 2 hours. Midway through the rise, deflate the dough by folding it in half. By the end of the rising time it will have increased in volume.

Dust the work surface. Divide the dough into 4 equal pieces and shape them into balls. Cover with a damp cloth and leave to rest for 15 minutes.

Working with 1 piece of dough at a time, use the palm of your hand to flatten it gently into a rough oval and top with 3–4 strips of orange peel. Fold a third of the dough in towards the center and press along the edge with your fingertips. Swivel the dough 180 degrees. Top with another 3–4 strips of orange peel, then fold in the other long edge so that it overlaps in the center and press again. Fold one half on top of the other and seal the edges together with the heel of your hand. Take hold of the ends of the dough and twist gently. Shape the other 3 loaves the same way.

Butter the loaf pans and the lids and lift in the twisted dough pieces, compressing them slightly to fit. Cover with a damp cloth and leave to proof for 1 hour.

Place a baking sheet on the bottom shelf of the oven and preheat to 450°F (230°C). Just before putting the loaves in the oven, pour 50 g (scant ¼ cup) of water onto the preheated baking sheet. Put the lids on the loaf pans and bake for 30 minutes.

Remove from the oven, turn out the loaves, and leave them to cool on a wire rack.

Breads with Extras

FIG BREAD

Makes 4 loaves,
each about 290 g

TIMINGS

- Mixing & kneading: 15 min
- First rising: 1 h 30 min
- Resting: 15 min
- Proofing: 1 h
- Baking: 20 min

INGREDIENTS

- 500 g (4 cups) all-purpose (plain) flour, plus extra for dusting
- 320 g (generous 1 1/4 cups) water at 68°F (20°C)
- 100 g (scant 1/2 cup) liquid sourdough starter (or 25 g [3 tablespoons] dry sourdough starter)
- 5 g (1 1/2 teaspoons) fresh baker's yeast, crumbled
- 10 g (2 teaspoons) salt
- 20 g (1 1/2 tablespoons) softened butter
- 200 g dried figs, roughly chopped

KNEADING IN A STAND MIXER

Place the flour, water, starter, fresh yeast, and salt in the bowl. Knead with the dough hook for 5 minutes at low speed, then for 10 minutes at high speed. Around 2 minutes before the end of the kneading time mix in the butter [1]. Switch off the machine, add the fig pieces [2], and then mix in briefly at low speed so as not to break them.

KNEADING BY HAND

Put the flour on a work surface or in a mixing bowl and make a large well in the center. Pour in half the water, the starter, fresh yeast, and salt. Mix well, then add the rest of the water and blend until all the flour has been incorporated. Add the butter and knead the dough until it becomes smooth and elastic. Towards the end of the kneading process, gently knead in the fig pieces.

Shape the dough into a ball and cover with a damp cloth. Leave to rise for 1 hour 30 minutes, by which time the dough will have increased in volume.

Dust the work surface. Divide the dough into 4 equal pieces and shape them into balls. Cover with a damp cloth and leave to rest for 15 minutes.

Working with 1 piece of dough at a time, use the palm of your hand to flatten it gently into a rough oval. With the long side facing you, fold in a third towards the center and press along the edge with your fingertips. Swivel the dough 180 degrees. Fold in the other long edge so that it overlaps in the center and press again. Fold one half on top of the other to create a plump oval shape and seal the edges together with the heel of your hand. Shape the other 3 loaves the same way.

Place the loaves on a baking sheet lined with parchment (baking) paper, seams underneath. Cover with a damp cloth and leave to proof for 1 hour.

Place another baking sheet on the bottom shelf of the oven and preheat to 450°F (230°C). Score each loaf in a crosshatch pattern [3]. Just before putting the loaves in the oven, pour 50 g (scant 1/4 cup) of water onto the preheated baking sheet. Bake for 20 minutes.

Remove the loaves from the oven and leave to cool on a wire rack.

183   Breads with Extras

HONEY BREAD

Makes 3 loaves,
each about 350 g

TIMINGS

- Mixing & kneading: 10 min
- First rising: 1h 30 min
- Resting: 15 min
- Proofing: 1h 30 min
- Baking: 20 min

INGREDIENTS

- 250 g (2 cups) all-purpose (plain) flour, plus extra for dusting
- 250 g (2 1/2 cups) light rye flour
- 300 g (1 1/4 cups) water at 68°F (20°C)
- 100 g (scant 1/2 cup) liquid sourdough starter (or 25 g [3 tablespoons] dry sourdough starter)
- 3 g (1 teaspoon) fresh baker's yeast, crumbled
- 10 g (2 teaspoons) salt
- 150 g (2/3 cup) clear honey, plus 3 extra teaspoons for topping

KNEADING IN A STAND MIXER

Put the 2 flours, water, starter, fresh yeast, salt, and honey in the bowl. Knead with the dough hook for 4 minutes at low speed, then for 6 minutes at high speed.

KNEADING BY HAND

Put the 2 flours on a work surface or in a mixing bowl and make a large well in the center. Pour in half the water, then add the starter, fresh yeast, salt, and honey. Mix well, then add the rest of the water and blend until all the flour has been incorporated. Knead the dough until it becomes smooth and elastic.

Shape into a ball and cover with a damp cloth. Leave to rise for 1 hour 30 minutes. Midway through the rise, deflate the dough by folding it in half. It will have increased in volume by the end of the rising time.

Dust the work surface. Divide the dough into 3 equal pieces and shape them into balls. Cover with a damp cloth and leave to rest for 15 minutes.

Turn the dough pieces around on the work surface and bring the edges in towards the center. Turn them again and shape into tight balls.

Place the loaves on a baking sheet lined with parchment (baking) paper, seams underneath. Cover with a damp cloth and leave to proof for 1 hour 30 minutes.

Place another baking sheet on the bottom shelf of the oven and preheat to 450°F (230°C).

Use your finger to create a small cavity in the center of each loaf, then score a large square in the surface around it (see page 39). Drop a teaspoon of honey into each cavity. Just before putting the loaves in the oven, pour 50 g (a scant 1/4 cup) of water onto the preheated baking sheet. Bake for 20 minutes.

Remove from the oven and leave to cool on a wire rack.

△ Instead of dusting the work surface before shaping the dough, oil it lightly with sunflower oil. Turn the dough around as above and bring the edges in towards the center, then transfer to a baking sheet and continue with the rising and baking, as above.

Breads with Extras

WALNUT & BUTTER BREAD

Makes 5 loaves,
each about 220 g

TIMINGS

- Mixing & kneading: 15 min
- First rising: 1h 30 min
- Resting: 15 min
- Proofing: 1h 15 min
- Baking: 17 min

INGREDIENTS

- 500 g (4 cups) all-purpose (plain) flour, plus extra for dusting
- 225 g (scant 1 cup) water at 68°F (20°C)
- 100 g (scant ½ cup) liquid sourdough starter (or 25 g [3 tablespoons] dry sourdough starter)
- 5 g (1½ teaspoons) fresh baker's yeast, crumbled
- 10 g (2 teaspoons) salt
- 25 g (¼ cup) milk powder
- 35 g (scant ¼ cup) sugar
- 75 g (⅓ cup) softened butter
- 150 g (1½ cups) walnuts, chopped

KNEADING IN A STAND MIXER

Put the flour, water, starter, fresh yeast, salt, milk powder and sugar in the bowl. Knead with the dough hook for 5 minutes at low speed [1], then for 7 minutes at high speed. Mix in the butter [2] and knead for another 3 minutes. Add the walnuts and mix in briefly at low speed.

KNEADING BY HAND

Put the flour on a work surface or in a mixing bowl and make a large well in the center. Pour in half the water, then add the starter, fresh yeast, salt, milk powder, and sugar. Mix well, then add the rest of the water and blend until all the flour has been incorporated. Add the butter and knead the dough until it becomes smooth and elastic. Add the walnuts at the end of the kneading.

Shape the dough into a ball, cover with a damp cloth, and leave to rise for 1 hour 30 minutes. Midway through the rise, deflate the dough by folding it in half. It will have increased in volume by the end of the rising time.

Dust the work surface. Divide the dough into 5 equal pieces and shape them into balls. Cover with a damp cloth and leave to rest for 15 minutes.

Working with 1 piece of dough at a time, use the palm of your hand to flatten it gently into a rough oval. With the long side facing you, fold in a third towards the center and press along the edge with your fingertips. Swivel the dough 180 degrees. Fold in the other long edge so that it overlaps in the center and press again. Fold one half on top of the other and seal the edges together with the heel of your hand [3]. With lightly floured hands, roll the dough out to form a plump oval. Shape the other 4 loaves the same way.

Score the loaves diagonally in a "sausage" cut [4] (see page 41). Place them, seams underneath, on a floured baker's cloth. Separate them by making folds in the cloth. Cover with a damp cloth and leave to proof for 1 hour 15 minutes.

Place a baking sheet on the bottom shelf of the oven and preheat to 450°F (230°C). Arrange the loaves on another baking sheet lined with parchment (baking) paper. Just before putting the loaves in the oven, pour 50 g (scant ¼ cup) of water onto the preheated baking sheet. Bake for 17 minutes.

Remove from the oven and leave to cool on a wire rack.

Breads with Extras

Walnut & Butter Bread   188

Breads with Extras

TURMERIC BREAD

Makes 4 loaves,
each about 250 g

TIMINGS
- Mixing & kneading: 15 min
- First rising: 1 h 30 min
- Resting: 15 min
- Proofing: 1 h
- Baking: 17 min

INGREDIENTS
- 500 g (4 cups) all-purpose (plain) flour, plus extra for dusting
- 250 g (1 cup) water at 68°F (20°C)
- 100 g (scant ½ cup) liquid sourdough starter (or 25 g [3 tablespoons] dry sourdough starter)
- 5 g (1½ teaspoons) fresh baker's yeast, crumbled
- 10 g (2 teaspoons) salt
- 25 g (¼ cup) milk powder
- 35 g (scant ¼ cup) sugar
- 75 g (⅓ cup) softened butter
- 5 g (2¼ teaspoons) ground turmeric

KNEADING IN A STAND MIXER
Put the flour, water, starter, fresh yeast, salt, milk powder, and sugar in the bowl. Knead with the dough hook for 5 minutes at low speed, then for 7 minutes at high speed. Mix in the butter and knead for another 3 minutes, then add the turmeric and mix well.

KNEADING BY HAND
Put the flour on a work surface or in a mixing bowl and make a large well in the center. Pour in half the water, then add the starter, the fresh yeast, salt, powdered milk, and sugar. Mix, then add the rest of the water and blend until all the flour has been incorporated. Next, incorporate the butter and turmeric and knead the dough until it becomes smooth and elastic.

Shape the dough into a ball, cover it with a damp cloth, and leave to rise for 1 hour 30 minutes. Midway through the rise, deflate the dough by folding it in half. It will have increased in volume by the end of the rising time.

Dust the work surface. Divide the dough into 4 equal pieces and shape them into balls. Cover with a damp cloth and leave to rest for 15 minutes.

Working with 1 piece of dough at a time, use the palm of your hand to flatten it gently to a rough oval. With the long side facing you, fold in a third towards the center and press along the edge with your fingertips. Swivel the dough 180 degrees. Fold in the other long edge so that it overlaps in the center and press again. Fold one half on top of the other and seal the edges together with the heel of your hand. With lightly floured hands, roll the dough out to form a plump oval. Shape the other 3 loaves the same way.

Place the loaves on a baking sheet lined with parchment (baking) paper, seams underneath. Cover with a damp cloth and leave to proof for 1 hour.

Place another baking sheet on the bottom shelf of the oven and preheat to 450°F (230°C). Score the loaves in a chevron pattern (see page 41), leaving a finger's width between the 2 rows of slashes. Just before putting the loaves in the oven, pour 50 g (scant ¼ cup) of water onto the preheated baking sheet. Bake for 17 minutes.

Remove from the oven and leave to cool on a wire rack.

Breads with Extras

MIXED FRUIT & NUT CROWNS

Makes 2 crowns,
each about 600 g

TIMINGS
• Mixing & kneading: 15min
• First rising: 1h 30min
• Resting: 15min
• Proofing: 2h
• Baking: 10min + 20min

INGREDIENTS
• 280 g mixed fruit and nuts
  (or 30% of the weight
  of the dough): your choice
  of raisins, currants, dried
  figs, cranberries, apricots,
  prunes, hazelnuts, pecans,
  almonds, cashews, pine
  nuts, or pistachios
• 500 g (4 cups) all-purpose
  (plain) flour, plus extra
  for dusting
• 325 g (1⅓ cups) water
  at 68°F (20°C)
• 100 g (scant ½ cup)
  liquid sourdough starter
  (or 25 g [3 tablespoons]
  dry sourdough starter)
• 5 g (1½ teaspoons) fresh
  baker's yeast, crumbled
• 10 g (2 teaspoons) salt
• 30 g (2 tablespoons)
  softened butter

Preheat the oven to 475°F (240°C). Spread your choice of mixed nuts out on a baking sheet lined with parchment (baking) paper and toast for 10 minutes [1]. Chop the larger ones roughly.

Cut the larger fruits (figs, prunes, and apricots) into smallish dice [2]. Mix all the dried fruit and nuts together in a mixing bowl [3].

KNEADING IN A STAND MIXER
Put the flour, water, starter, fresh yeast, and salt in the bowl. Knead with the dough hook for 5 minutes at low speed, then for 7 minutes at high speed. Mix in the butter and knead for another 3 minutes. Add the dried fruit and nuts and mix in briefly at low speed.

KNEADING BY HAND
Put the flour on a work surface or in a mixing bowl and make a large well in the center. Pour in half the water, then add the starter, fresh yeast, and salt. Mix well, then add the rest of the water and knead until all the flour has been incorporated. Add the butter, then knead the dough until it becomes smooth and elastic. Add the fruit and nuts toward the end of the kneading time.

Shape the dough into a ball and cover it with a damp cloth. Leave to rise for 1 hour 30 minutes. It will have increased in volume by the end of the rising time [4].

Dust the work surface. Divide the dough into 2 equal pieces and shape them into balls. Cover with a damp cloth and leave to rest for 15 minutes.

Working with 1 piece of dough at a time, use your fingers to make a large hole right through the center [5, 6]. Working carefully [7], stretch and pull the dough as evenly as you can, to make the crown larger and larger [8, 9, 10], until it reaches a diameter of around 12 inches (30 cm). Shape the second crown in the same way.

Place the crowns in floured banneton rings (the type known as *couronnes*) [11]. Alternatively, sit a small bowl inside a large banneton and drape with a cloth to approximate the *couronne*. Cover with a damp cloth and leave to proof for 2 hours.

Place a baking sheet on the bottom shelf of the oven and preheat to 450°F (230°C). Turn the crowns out onto 2 more baking sheets lined with parchment (baking) paper. Score them however you like [12]. Just before putting the crowns in the oven, pour 50 g (scant ¼ cup) of water onto the preheated baking sheet. Bake for 20 minutes.

Remove from the oven and leave to cool on a wire rack.

1

2

3

4

5

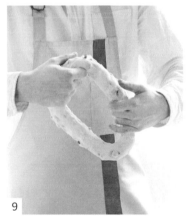

6

7

8

9

10

11

12

Breads with Extras

Mixed Fruit & Nut Crowns   194

Breads with Extras

SESAME SEED BREAD

Makes 4 loaves,
each about 300 g

TIMINGS

- Steeping: 2–3h
- Mixing & kneading: 15min
- First rising: 2h
- Resting: 15min
- Proofing: 1h 30min
- Baking: 10min + 18min

INGREDIENTS

- 200 g (1 1/3 cup)
  sesame seeds, plus extra
  for topping
- 70 g (generous 1/4 cup)
  water
- 500 g (4 cups) all-purpose
  (plain) flour, plus extra
  for dusting
- 325 g (1 1/3 cups) water
  at 68°F (20°C)
- 100 g (scant 1/2 cup)
  liquid sourdough starter
  (or 25 g [3 tablespoons]
  dry sourdough starter)
- 5 g (1 1/2 teaspoons) fresh
  baker's yeast, crumbled
- 10 g (2 teaspoons) salt

Preheat the oven to 475°F (240°C). Spread the sesame seeds out on a baking sheet lined with parchment (baking) paper and toast for 10 minutes [1]. Add 100 g (2/3 cup) of toasted seeds to a bowl with the water and leave to steep for 2–3 hours [2].

KNEADING IN A STAND MIXER

Put the flour, water, starter, fresh yeast, and salt in the bowl. Knead with the dough hook for 5 minutes at low speed, then for 10 minutes at high speed. Towards the end of the kneading time, add the sesame seeds, together with the steeping water.

KNEADING BY HAND

Put the flour on a work surface or in a mixing bowl and make a large well in the center. Pour in half the water, then add the starter, fresh yeast, and salt. Mix well, then add the rest of the water and blend until all the flour has been incorporated. Add the sesame seeds, together with the steeping water. Knead the dough until it becomes smooth and elastic.

Shape the dough into a ball, cover with a damp cloth, and leave to rise for 2 hours. Midway through the rise, deflate the dough by folding it in half. It will have increased in volume by the end of the rising time.

Dust the work surface. Divide the dough into 4 equal pieces and shape them into balls. Cover with a damp cloth and leave to rest for 15 minutes.

Working with 1 piece of dough at a time, use the palm of your hand to flatten it gently into a rough oval. With the long side facing you, fold in a third towards the center and press along the edge with your fingertips. Swivel the dough 180 degrees. Fold in the other long edge so that it overlaps in the center and press again. Fold one half on top of the other and seal the edges together with the heel of your hand. Shape the other 3 loaves the same way.

Cover a plate with extra sesame seeds (not soaked). Use a dough scraper to slice the dough pieces in half lengthwise. Take hold of the ends of each piece of dough and twist gently. Brush or spray lightly with water, then press the tops of the loaves in the sesame seeds to coat evenly [3].

Place the loaves on a baking sheet lined with parchment (baking) paper. Cover with a damp cloth and leave to proof for 1 hour 30 minutes.

Place another baking sheet on the bottom shelf of the oven and preheat to 450°F (230°C). Slash the top of each loaf twice. Just before putting the loaves in the oven, pour 50 g (scant 1/4 cup) of water onto the preheated baking sheet. Bake for 18 minutes. Remove from the oven and leave to cool on a wire rack.

CUTTLE-FISH INK BREAD

Makes 3 loaves,
each about 310 g

TIMINGS

- Mixing & kneading: 16 min
- First resting: 1 h
- First rising: 45 min
- Second resting: 30 min
- Proofing: 3 h
- Baking: 20 min

INGREDIENTS

- 500 g (4 cups) all-purpose (plain) flour, plus extra for dusting
- 300 g (1¼ cups) water at 68°F (20°C)
- 100 g (scant ½ cup) liquid sourdough starter (or 25 g [3 tablespoons] dry sourdough starter)
- 3 g (1 teaspoon) fresh baker's yeast, crumbled
- 10 g (2 teaspoons) salt
- 10 g (1 tablespoon) cuttlefish or squid ink

KNEADING IN A STAND MIXER

Put the flour and water in the bowl. Mix for 5 minutes at low speed. Remove the bowl from the machine and cover it with a lightly damp cloth. Leave to rest for 1 hour, then add the starter, fresh yeast, salt, and cuttlefish ink. Knead with the dough hook for 4 minutes at low speed, then for 7 minutes at high speed.

KNEADING BY HAND

Put the flour on a work surface or in a mixing bowl and make a large well in the center. Pour in two-thirds of the water and mix until all the flour has been incorporated. Cover with a damp cloth and leave to rest for 1 hour. Add the rest of the water, the starter, fresh yeast, salt, and cuttlefish ink. Knead the dough until it becomes smooth and elastic.

Shape the dough into a ball and cover with a damp cloth. Leave to rise for 45 minutes. It will have increased in volume by the end of the rising time.

Dust the work surface with flour. Divide the dough into 3 equal pieces. Fold each piece over on itself, pulling gently to stretch into a log. Cover with a damp cloth and leave to rest for 30 minutes.

Use a dough scraper to cut each log lengthwise in thirds so you have a total of 9 smaller pieces. Stretch and roll each piece gently to form strips, around 12 inches (30 cm) long and ½-¾ inches (1.5-2 cm) in diameter, slightly thicker in the center.

Take 3 strips and join them together at one end. Braid the 3 strips together until you reach the end. Seal firmly. Make 2 other braids in the same way.

Place the braids on a baking sheet lined with parchment (baking) paper. Cover with a damp cloth and leave to proof for 3 hours.

Place another baking sheet on the bottom shelf of the oven and preheat to 450°F (230°C). Just before putting the braids in the oven, pour 50 g (scant ¼ cup) of water onto the preheated baking sheet. Bake for 20 minutes.

Remove from the oven and leave to cool on a wire rack.

Breads with Extras

OIL-ENRICHED
BREADS

PLAIN CIABATTA

Makes four ciabattas,
each about 240 g

TIMINGS
- Mixing & kneading: 15 min
- First rising: 2 h
- Resting: 15 min
- Proofing: 1 h
- Baking: 16 min

INGREDIENTS
- 500 g (4 cups) all-purpose (plain) flour, plus extra for dusting
- 320 g (generous 1¼ cups) water at 68°F (20°C)
- 100 g (scant ½ cup) liquid sourdough starter (or 25 g [3 tablespoons] dry sourdough starter)
- 5 g (1½ teaspoons) fresh baker's yeast, crumbled
- 10 g (2 teaspoons) salt
- 30 g (2 tablespoons) extra-virgin olive oil, plus extra for brushing

KNEADING IN A STAND MIXER
Put the flour, water, starter, fresh yeast, and salt in the bowl. Knead with the dough hook for 5 minutes at low speed, then for 8 minutes at high speed. Add the olive oil and knead for another 2 minutes on high speed.

KNEADING BY HAND
Put the flour on a work surface or in a mixing bowl and make a large well in the center [1]. Pour in half the water [2], mix well and then add the starter [3], fresh yeast, and salt. Start kneading with one hand [4], while using the other to gradually bring the flour into the center. Add the rest of the water little by little, followed by the oil [5], and continue kneading until all the flour has been incorporated [6]. Take the dough in both hands [7], throw it forcefully onto the work surface [8], then fold it forward. Repeat this throwing and folding until the dough becomes smooth and elastic.

Shape the dough into a ball [9] and cover it with a damp cloth. Leave to rise for 2 hours. Midway through the rise, deflate the dough by folding it in half. By the end of the rising time it will have increased in volume [10].

Dust the work surface. Divide the dough into four equal pieces [11]. Fold each piece over on itself, pulling gently to stretch into a log. Cover with a damp cloth and leave to rest for 15 minutes.

Working with one piece of dough at a time, use the palm of your hand to flatten it gently. With the long side facing you, fold in a third of the dough towards the center and press along the edge with your fingertips. Fold in the other long edge so that it overlaps in the center and press the edges with your fingertips. Shape the other three loaves the same way.

Turn the loaves so the seams are underneath, then cover with a damp cloth and leave to proof for 1 hour.

Place a baking sheet on the bottom shelf of the oven and preheat to 460°F (235°C). Turn the loaves onto another baking sheet lined with parchment (baking) paper, seams on top. Just before putting them in the oven, pour 50 g (scant ¼ cup) of water onto the preheated baking sheet. Bake for 4 minutes, then lower the temperature to 425°F (220°C) and bake for another 12 minutes.

Remove from the oven, brush lightly with olive oil, and leave to cool on a wire rack.

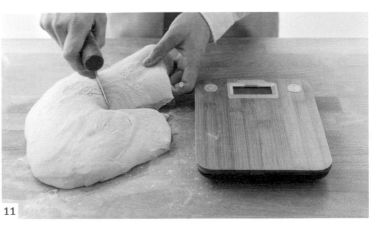

203   Oil-Enriched Breads

Oil-Enriched Breads

OLIVE OIL

Bread is made with olive oil all around the Mediterranean, wherever the olive tree flourishes. Nevertheless, it's the Italian *panini all'olio* that we tend to think of first, as they have eclipsed all other versions of olive-oil bread! French bakeries have long since adopted focaccia, which originated in Genoa, the Venetian ciabatta, and the *grissini*—or breadsticks—that appear on Italian table as an appetizer. The defining characteristics of all these breads derives from the addition of olive oil to the dough and to their high hydration level: this is what gives them such a melting, light texture. Try the Plain Ciabatta and its variations (pages 202-14), the Rosemary Focaccia (page 124) and its equivalents, which include not only the fougasses (pages 220-26), but also Pizza (page 228), Breadsticks (page 286), Basil Bread (page 216), and Sun-Dried Tomato Bread (page 286).

MIXED-SEED CIABATTA

Makes four ciabattas, each about 280 g

TIMINGS
- Steeping: 2h
- Mixing & kneading: 15min
- First rising: 2h
- Resting: 15min
- Proofing: 1h
- Baking: 10min + 15min

INGREDIENTS
- 90 g (¾ cup) mixed seeds: millet, pumpkin, and sesame, plus extra for topping
- 500 g (4 cups) all-purpose (plain) flour, plus extra for dusting
- 325 g (scant 1⅓ cups) water at 68°F (20°C) plus 60 g (¼ cup) for steeping the seeds
- 100 g (scant ½ cup) liquid sourdough starter (or 25 g [3 tablespoons] dry sourdough starter)
- 5 g (1½ teaspoons) fresh baker's yeast, crumbled
- 10 g (2 teaspoons) salt
- 30 g (2 tablespoons) extra-virgin olive oil, plus extra for brushing

Preheat the oven to 500°F (250°C). Spread the mixed seeds out on a baking sheet lined with parchment (baking) paper and toast for 10 minutes. Tip them immediately into a bowl with the 60 g (¼ cup) water and leave to steep for 2 hours. Drain away any water that remains.

KNEADING IN A STAND MIXER
Put the flour, water, starter, fresh yeast, and salt in the bowl. Knead with the dough hook for 5 minutes at low speed, then for 8 minutes at high speed. Add the olive oil and knead for another two minutes on high speed, then add the mixed seeds.

KNEADING BY HAND
Put the flour on a work surface or in a mixing bowl and make a large well in the center. Pour in half the water, the starter, fresh yeast, and salt. Mix well, then add the rest of the water, then the olive oil and mixed seeds, and blend until all the flour has been incorporated. Knead the dough until it becomes smooth and elastic.

Shape the dough into a ball, cover with a damp cloth and leave to rise for 2 hours. Midway through the rise, deflate the dough by folding it in half. By the end of the rising time it will have increased in volume.

Dust the work surface. Divide the dough into four equal pieces. Fold each piece over on itself, pulling gently to stretch into a log. Cover with a damp cloth and leave to rest for 15 minutes.

Working with one piece of dough at a time, use the palm of your hand to flatten it gently. With the long side facing you, fold in a third of the dough towards the center and press along the edge with your fingertips. Fold in the other long edge so that it overlaps in the center and press the edges with your fingertips. Shape the other three loaves the same way.

Cover a plate with extra mixed seeds (not soaked). Brush or spray the loaves lightly with water and press them in the seeds to coat the tops evenly. Transfer the loaves to a baking sheet lined with parchment (baking) paper, seams underneath. Cover with a damp cloth and leave to proof for 1 hour.

Place a baking sheet on the bottom shelf of the oven and preheat to 460°F (235°C). Just before putting the loaves in the oven, pour 50 g (scant ¼ cup) of water onto the preheated baking sheet. Bake for 4 minutes, then lower the temperature to 425°F (220°C) and bake for another 11 minutes.

Remove from the oven, brush lightly with olive oil, and leave to cool on a wire rack.

209   Oil-Enriched Breads

BUCK-WHEAT CIABATTA

Makes four ciabattas,
each about 240 g

TIMINGS
- Mixing & kneading: 15 min
- First rising: 2 h
- Resting: 15 min
- Proofing: 1 h
- Baking: 12 min

INGREDIENTS
- 450 g (3¾ cups) all-purpose (plain) flour, plus extra for dusting
- 50 g (⅓ cup) buckwheat flour
- 325 g (scant 1⅓ cups) water at 68°F (20°C)
- 100 g (scant ½ cup) liquid sourdough starter (or 25 g [3 tablespoons] dry sourdough starter)
- 3 g (1 teaspoon) fresh baker's yeast, crumbled
- 10 g (2 teaspoons) salt
- 30 g (2 tablespoons) extra-virgin olive oil, plus extra for brushing

KNEADING IN A STAND MIXER
Put the two flours, water, starter, fresh yeast, and salt in the bowl. Knead with the dough hook for 5 minutes at low speed, then for 7 minutes at high speed. Add the olive oil and knead for another 3 minutes at high speed.

KNEADING BY HAND
Put the two flours on a work surface or in a mixing bowl and make a large well in the center. Pour in half the water, the starter, fresh yeast, and salt. Mix well, then add the rest of the water and then the olive oil, and blend until all the flour has been incorporated. Knead the dough until it becomes smooth and elastic.

Shape the dough into a ball [1], cover with a damp cloth, and leave to rise for 2 hours. Midway through the rise, deflate the dough by folding it in half. By the end of the rising time it will have increased in volume.

Dust the work surface. Divide the dough into four equal pieces. Fold each piece over on itself, pulling gently to stretch into a log. Cover with a damp cloth and leave to rest for 15 minutes.

Working with one piece of dough at a time, use the palm of your hand to flatten it gently. With the long side facing you, fold in a third of the dough towards the center [2] and press along the edge with your fingertips. Fold in the other long edge so that it overlaps in the center [3] and press the edges together with your fingertips. Shape the other three loaves the same way.

Turn the loaves so the seams are underneath, then cover with a damp cloth and leave to proof for 1 hour.

Place a baking sheet on the bottom shelf of the oven and preheat to 460°F (235°C). Turn the loaves onto another baking sheet lined with parchment (baking) paper, seams on top. Just before putting them in the oven, pour 50 g (scant ¼ cup) of water onto the preheated baking sheet. Bake for 4 minutes, then lower the temperature to 425°F (220°C) and bake for another 8 minutes.

Remove from the oven, brush lightly with olive oil, and leave to cool on a wire rack.

Oil-Enriched Breads

PUMPKIN-SEED CIABATTA

Makes four ciabattas, each about 280 g

TIMINGS
- Steeping: 2 h
- Mixing & kneading: 15 min
- First rising: 2 h
- Resting: 15 min
- Proofing: 1 h
- Baking: 10 min + 15 min

INGREDIENTS
- 100 g (1 cup) pumpkin seeds, plus extra for topping
- 500 g (4 cups) all-purpose (plain) flour
- 320 g (generous 1 1/4 cups) water at 68°F (20°C), plus 70 g (generous 1/4 cup) for steeping
- 100 g (scant 1/2 cup) liquid sourdough starter (or 25 g [3 tablespoons] dry sourdough starter)
- 5 g (1 1/2 teaspoons) fresh baker's yeast, crumbled
- 10 g (2 teaspoons) salt
- 30 g (2 tablespoons) extra-virgin olive oil, plus extra for brushing

Preheat the oven to 500°F (250°C). Spread the pumpkin seeds out on a baking sheet lined with parchment (baking) paper and toast for 10 minutes. Tip them immediately into a bowl with the 70 g (generous 1/4 cup) water and leave to steep for 2 hours. Drain away any water that remains.

KNEADING IN A STAND MIXER
Put the flour, water, starter, fresh yeast, and salt in the bowl. Knead with the dough hook for 5 minutes at low speed, then for 7 minutes at high speed. Add the olive oil and knead for another 3 minutes on high speed. Add the steeped pumpkin seeds, and mix them in gently.

KNEADING BY HAND
Put the flour on a work surface or in a mixing bowl and make a large well in the center. Pour in half the water, then add the starter, fresh yeast, and salt. Mix well, then add the rest of the water, the olive oil, and the steeped pumpkin seeds and blend until all the flour has been incorporated. Knead the dough until it becomes smooth and elastic.

Shape the dough into a ball, cover with a damp cloth, and leave to rise for 2 hours. Midway through the rise, deflate the dough by folding it in half. By the end of the rising time it will have increased in volume.

Dust the work surface. Divide the dough into four equal pieces. Fold each piece over on itself, pulling gently to stretch into a log. Cover with a damp cloth and leave to rest for 15 minutes.

Working with one piece of dough at a time, use the palm of your hand to flatten it gently. With the long side facing you, fold in a third of the dough towards the center and press along the edge with your fingertips. Fold in the other long edge so that it overlaps in the center and press the edges with your fingertips [1]. Shape the other three loaves the same way.

Cover a plate with extra pumpkin seeds (not soaked). Brush or spray the tops of the loaves lightly with water and roll them in the seeds to coat evenly [2, 3]. Transfer the loaves to a baking sheet lined with parchment (baking) paper, seams underneath. Cover with a damp cloth and leave to proof for 1 hour.

Place a baking sheet on the bottom shelf of the oven and preheat to 460°F (235°C). Just before putting the loaves in the oven, pour 50 g (scant 1/4 cup) of water onto the preheated baking sheet. Bake for 4 minutes, lower the temperature to 425°F (220°C) and bake for another 11 minutes. Remove from the oven, brush lightly with olive oil, and leave them to cool on a wire rack.

213   Oil-Enriched Breads

ROUND CIABATTA

Divide the dough into four equal pieces. Working with one piece at a time, turn it around on the work surface, bring the edges in to the center and press down. Turn it again and shape into a ball, tucking the seam underneath [1].

Repeat with the other three pieces of dough, then cover them with a damp cloth and leave to rest for 15 minutes. Press each piece of dough gently, then brush or spray the tops with water [2].

Roll in pumpkin seeds [3] and continue with the proofing and baking as described in the main recipe [4].

215

BASIL BREAD

Makes four loaves,
each about 250 g

TIMINGS

- Steeping the basil: 6-12h
- Mixing & kneading: 15min
- First rising: 2h
- Resting: 15min
- Proofing: 1h
- Baking: 18min

INGREDIENTS

- 75g (scant 1 cup) basil leaves
- 30 g (2 tablespoons) extra-virgin olive oil, plus extra for brushing
- 500 g (4 cups) all-purpose (plain) flour
- 300 g (1¼ cups) water at 68°F (20°C)
- 100 g (scant ½ cup) liquid sourdough starter (or 25 g [3 tablespoons] dry sourdough starter)
- 3 g (1 teaspoon) fresh baker's yeast, crumbled
- 10 g (2 teaspoons) salt

The night before (or at least 6 hours ahead of time), coarsely chop the basil [1]. Mix with the olive oil and leave to steep overnight at room temperature [2].

KNEADING IN A STAND MIXER

Put the flour, water, starter, fresh yeast, and salt in the bowl. Knead with the dough hook for 5 minutes at low speed, then for 7 minutes at high speed. Add the basil oil and knead for another 3 minutes at high speed.

KNEADING BY HAND

Put the flour on a work surface or in a mixing bowl and make a large well in the center. Pour in half the water, then add the starter, fresh yeast, and salt. Mix well, then add the rest of the water and the basil oil and blend until all the flour has been incorporated. Knead the dough until it becomes smooth and elastic.

Shape the dough into a ball, cover with a damp cloth, and leave to rise for 2 hours. Midway through the rise, deflate the dough by folding it in half. By the end of the rising time it will have increased in volume.

Dust the work surface. Divide the dough into four equal pieces. Fold each piece over on itself, then roll into balls with the seams underneath. Cover with a damp cloth and leave to rest for 15 minutes.

Turn the balls of dough between your hands on a floured work surface [3], pressing down gently. Cover with a damp cloth and leave to proof for 1 hour. By the end of the proofing time they will have increased in volume [4].

Place a baking sheet on the bottom shelf of the oven and preheat to 460°F (235°C). Lift the balls of dough onto another baking sheet lined with parchment (baking) paper. Score them in a crosshatch pattern [5] (see page 39).

Just before putting the loaves in the oven, pour 50 g (scant ¼ cup) of water onto the preheated baking sheet. Bake for 4 minutes, then lower the temperature to 425°F (220°C) and bake for another 14 minutes.

Remove from the oven, brush lightly with olive oil, and leave to cool on a wire rack.

1

2

3

4

5

Oil-Enriched Breads

SUN-DRIED TOMATO BREAD

Makes four loaves,
each about 270 g

TIMINGS
- Mixing & kneading: 15 min
- First rising: 2 h
- Resting: 15 min
- Proofing: 1 h
- Baking: 15 min

INGREDIENTS
- 500 g (4 cups) all-purpose (plain) flour
- 300 g (1¼ cups) water at 68°F (20°C)
- 100 g (scant ½ cup) liquid sourdough starter (or 25 g [3 tablespoons] dry sourdough starter)
- 3 g (1 teaspoon) fresh baker's yeast, crumbled
- 10 g (2 teaspoons) salt
- 30 g (2 tablespoons) extra-virgin olive oil, plus extra for brushing
- 150 g (3 cups) sun-dried tomatoes in oil, chopped

KNEADING IN A STAND MIXER
Put the flour, water, starter, fresh yeast, and salt in the bowl. Knead with the dough hook for 5 minutes at low speed, then for 7 minutes at high speed. Add the olive oil and knead for another 3 minutes. Add the sun-dried tomatoes at the end and mix at low speed.

KNEADING BY HAND
Put the flour on a work surface or in a mixing bowl and make a large well in the center. Pour in half the water, then add the starter, fresh yeast, and salt. Mix well, then add the rest of the water and the olive oil, and blend until all the flour has been incorporated. Knead the dough until it becomes smooth and elastic. Add the sun-dried tomatoes towards the end of the kneading time.

Shape the dough into a ball, cover with a damp cloth, and leave to rise for 2 hours. Midway through the rise, deflate the dough by folding it in half. By the end of the rising time it will have increased in volume.

Dust the work surface. Divide the dough into four equal pieces [1]. Fold each piece over on itself [2], then roll into balls [3] with the seams underneath. Cover with a damp cloth and leave to rest for 15 minutes.

Working with one piece of dough at a time, use the palm of your hand to flatten it gently to a rough oval. With the long side facing you, fold in a third towards the center and press along the edge with your fingertips. Swivel the dough 180 degrees. Fold in the other long edge so that it overlaps in the center and press again. Fold one half on top of the other and seal the edges together with the heel of your hand. With lightly floured hands, roll the dough out to form a plump oval. Shape the other three loaves the same way.

Place the pieces of dough on a baking sheet lined with parchment (baking) paper, seams underneath. Score the loaves diagonally in a "sausage" cut (see page 41). Cover with a damp cloth and leave to proof for 1 hour.

Place a baking sheet on the bottom shelf of the oven and preheat to 460°F (235°C). Arrange the loaves on another baking sheet lined with parchment (baking) paper. Just before putting the loaves in the oven, pour 50 g (a scant ¼ cup) of water onto the preheated baking sheet. Bake for 4 minutes, then lower the temperature to 425°F (220°C) and bake for another for 11 minutes.

Remove from the oven, brush with olive oil, and leave to cool on a wire rack.

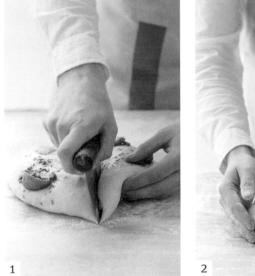

1

2

3

Oil-Enriched Breads

FOUGASSE WITH ASH GOAT CHEESE

Makes four fougasses, each about 330 g

TIMINGS
- Mixing & kneading: 15 min
- First rising: 2h
- Resting: 15 min
- Proofing: 1h
- Baking: 18 min

INGREDIENTS
- 500 g (4 cups) all-purpose (plain) flour, plus extra for dusting
- 300 g (1¼ cups) water at 68°F (20°C)
- 100 g (scant ½ cup) liquid sourdough starter (or 25 g [3 tablespoons] dry sourdough starter)
- 5 g (1½ teaspoons) fresh baker's yeast, crumbled
- 10 g (2 teaspoons) salt
- 30 g (2 tablespoons) extra-virgin olive oil, plus extra for brushing
- 200 g (scant ¼ cup) ash goat cheese
- 100 g (scant ½ cup) crème fraîche
- 100 g (scant 1 cup) grated Swiss cheese (Emmental)

KNEADING IN A STAND MIXER
Put the flour, water, starter, fresh yeast, and salt in the bowl. Knead with the dough hook for 5 minutes at low speed, then for 7 minutes at high speed. Add the olive oil and knead for another 3 minutes.

KNEADING BY HAND
Put the flour on a work surface or in a mixing bowl and make a large well in the center. Pour in half the water, then add the starter, fresh yeast, and salt. Mix well, then add the rest of the water and the olive oil and blend until all the flour has been incorporated. Knead the dough until it becomes smooth and elastic.

Shape the dough into a ball, cover with a damp cloth, and leave to rise for 2 hours. Midway through the rise, deflate the dough by folding it in half. By the end of the rising time it will have increased in volume.

Dust the work surface. Divide the dough into four equal pieces. Working with one piece at a time, turn it around on the work surface, bring the edges in to the center, and press down. Turn it again and shape into a ball, tucking the seam underneath. Repeat with the other three pieces of dough, then cover them with a damp cloth and leave to rest for 15 minutes.

Cut the goat cheese into slices. Use a rolling pin to roll each piece of dough into oval flatbreads, around 16 inches (40 cm) long and about ¼ inch (5 mm) thick. Spread one half of each flatbread with crème fraîche, leaving a ¾-inch (2-cm) border around the edge. Sprinkle with Swiss cheese (Emmental) and top with slices of goat cheese [1].

Use a dough-cutter to make 3 wide slashes on the ungarnished half of each flatbread [2], then fold it over the other half [3]. Seal all the edges.

Place the fougasses on lightly oiled baking sheets. Cover with a damp cloth and leave to proof for 1 hour.

Place a baking sheet on the bottom shelf of the oven and preheat to 460°F (235°C). Just before putting the loaves in the oven, pour 50 g (scant ¼ cup) of water onto the preheated baking sheet. Bake the fougasses for 4 minutes, then lower the temperature to 425°F (220°C) and continue bake for another 14 minutes.

Remove from the oven, brush lightly with olive oil, and leave to cool on a wire rack.

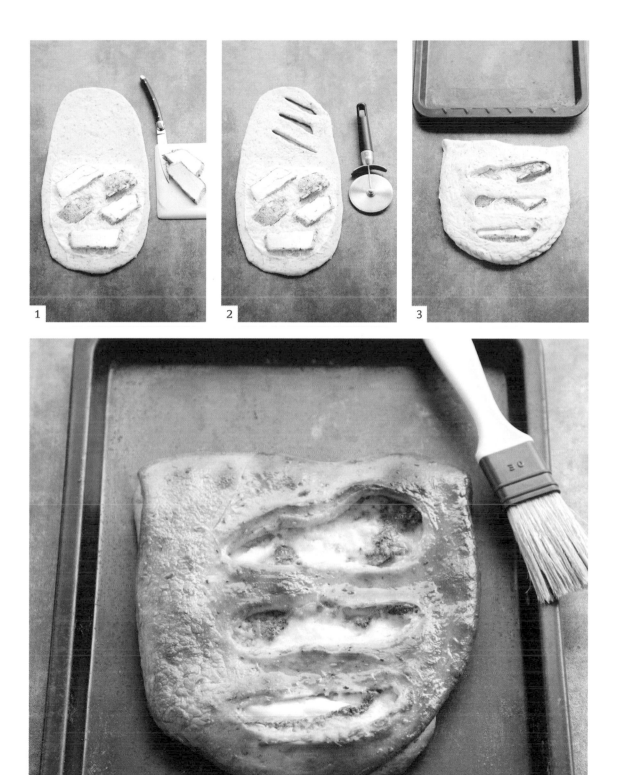

Oil-Enriched Breads

FOUGASSE WITH BLACK & GREEN OLIVES

Makes four fougasses, each about 300 g

TIMINGS
- Mixing & kneading: 15 min
- First rising: 2h
- Resting: 15 min
- Proofing: 1h
- Baking: 13 min

INGREDIENTS
- 500 g (4 cups) all-purpose (plain) flour, plus extra for dusting
- 320 g (generous 1¼ cups) water at 68°F (20°C)
- 100 g (scant ½ cup) liquid sourdough starter (or 25 g [3 tablespoons] dry sourdough starter)
- 5 g (1½ teaspoons) fresh baker's yeast, crumbled
- 10 g (2 teaspoons) salt
- 30 g (2 tablespoons) extra-virgin olive oil, plus extra for brushing
- 200 g (1⅔ cups) pitted black and green olives, whole or sliced, plus extra for decoration
- 100 g (scant 1 cup) grated Swiss cheese (Emmental)

KNEADING IN A STAND MIXER
Put the flour, water, starter, fresh yeast, and salt in the bowl. Knead with the dough hook for 5 minutes at low speed, then for 7 minutes at high speed. Add the olive oil and knead for another 3 minutes. Turn off the machine, add the olives, and mix again at low speed [1].

KNEADING BY HAND
Put the flour on a work surface or in a mixing bowl and make a large well in the center. Pour in half the water, then add the starter, fresh yeast, and salt. Mix well, then add the rest of the water and the olive oil and blend until all the flour has been incorporated. Knead the dough until it becomes smooth and elastic. Add the olives toward the end of the kneading time.

Shape the dough into a ball, cover with a damp cloth, and leave to rise for 2 hours. Midway through the rise, deflate the dough by folding it in half. By the end of the rising time it will have increased in volume [2].

Dust the work surface. Divide the dough into four equal pieces [3]. Fold each piece over on itself to lengthen [4]. Cover with a damp cloth and leave to rest for 15 minutes.

Use a rolling pin to roll each piece of dough into oval flatbreads, around 8 inches (20 cm) long and about ¾ inch (2 cm) thick [5, 6, 7]. Brush them with water [8]. Sprinkle the Swiss cheese (Emmental) onto the work surface. Press each piece of dough into the cheese to coat evenly, then transfer to baking sheets lined with parchment (baking) paper [9].

Use a dough cutter to score long cuts into each flatbread in a leaf or wheat sheaf design [10]. Stretch the cuts gently to widen and emphasise the holes [11, 12] which will prevent them from closing up as they bake.

Decorate the fougasses with the extra olives. Cover them with a damp cloth and leave to proof for 1 hour.

Place a baking sheet on the bottom shelf of the oven and preheat to 460°F (235°C). Just before putting the loaves in the oven, pour 50 g (scant ¼ cup) of water onto the preheated baking sheet. Bake the fougasses for 4 minutes, then lower the temperature to 425°F (220°C) and continue bake for another 9 minutes.

Remove from the oven, brush lightly with olive oil, and leave them to cool on a wire rack.

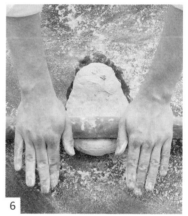

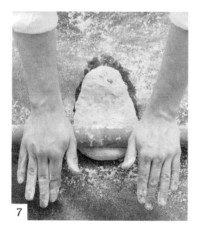

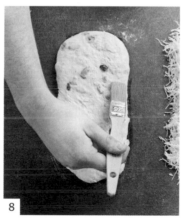

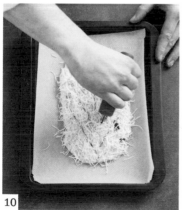

223   Oil-Enriched Breads

Fougasse with Black & Green Olives   224

Oil-Enriched Breads

FOUGASSE WITH LARDONS

Makes four fougasses, each about 340 g

TIMINGS
- Mixing & kneading: 15 min
- First rising: 2 h
- Resting: 15 min
- Proofing: 1 h
- Baking: 14 min

INGREDIENTS
- 250 g smoked lardons or pancetta
- 500 g (4 cups) all-purpose (plain) flour, plus extra for dusting
- 300 g (1 1/4 cups) water at 68°F (20°C)
- 100 g (scant 1/2 cup) liquid sourdough starter (or 25 g [3 tablespoons] dry sourdough starter)
- 5 g (1 1/2 teaspoons) fresh baker's yeast, crumbled
- 10 g (2 teaspoons) salt
- 30 g (2 tablespoons) extra-virgin olive oil, plus extra for brushing
- 100 g (scant 1/2 cup) crème fraîche
- 75 g (3/4 cup) grated Swiss cheese (Emmental)

Brown the lardons in a frying pan over medium heat. Drain in a sieve lined with paper towels.

KNEADING IN A STAND MIXER
Put the flour, water, starter, fresh yeast, and salt in the bowl. Knead with the dough hook for 5 minutes at low speed, then for 10 minutes at high speed. Add the olive oil 3 minutes before the end of the kneading time].

KNEADING BY HAND
Put the flour on a work surface or in a mixing bowl and make a large well in the center. Pour in half the water, starter, fresh yeast, and salt. Mix well, then add the remaining water and the olive oil and blend until all the flour has been incorporated. Knead the dough until it is smooth and elastic.

Shape the dough into a ball, cover with a damp cloth, and leave to rise for 2 hours. Midway through the rise, deflate the dough by folding it in half. By the end of the rising time it will have increased in volume.

Dust the work surface. Divide the dough into four equal pieces. Fold each piece over on itself to lengthen. Cover with a damp cloth and leave to rest for 15 minutes.

Use a rolling pin to roll each piece of dough into oval flatbreads, around 8 inches (20 cm) long and about 3/4 inch (2 cm) thick [2].

Place the flatbreads in pairs on baking sheets lined with parchment (baking) paper. Spread each one with crème fraîche, leaving a 1/2-inch (1-cm) border around the edge. Sprinkle with Swiss cheese (Emmental) and top with lardons [3]. Leave to proof for at least 1 hour.

Place a baking sheet on the bottom shelf of the oven and preheat to 460°F (235°C). Just before putting the loaves in the oven, pour 50 g (scant 1/4 cup) of water onto the preheated baking sheet. Bake the fougasses for 4 minutes, then lower the temperature to 425°F (220°C) and bake for another 10 minutes.

Remove from the oven and brush the border of each fougasse lightly with olive oil.

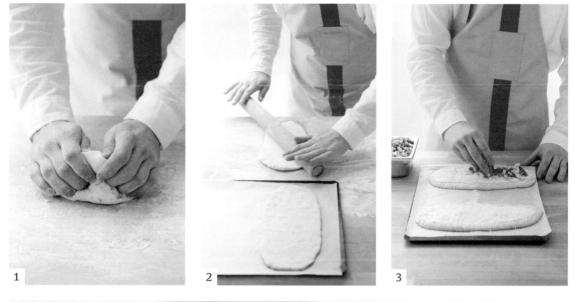

227   Oil-Enriched Breads

PIZZA

Makes two large pizzas

TIMINGS
- Mixing & kneading: 13 min
- First rising: 2 h
- Proofing: 1 h
- Baking: 15 min

INGREDIENTS
- 500 g (4 cups) all-purpose (plain) flour, plus extra for dusting
- 260 g (1 cup water) at 68°F (20°C)
- 100 g (scant ½ cup) liquid sourdough starter (or 25 g [3 tablespoons] dry sourdough starter)
- 5 g (1½ teaspoons) fresh baker's yeast, crumbled
- 15 g (1 tablespoon) superfine (caster) sugar
- 10 g (2 teaspoons) salt
- 30 g (2 tablespoons) extra-virgin olive oil

For the topping:
- 400 g (1⅔ cups) fresh tomato sauce
- 10 slices of ham, halved or cut into strips
- fresh or dried oregano
- 200 g (1⅔ cups) grated Swiss cheese (Emmental)

KNEADING IN A STAND MIXER
Put the flour, water, starter, fresh yeast, sugar, and salt in the bowl. Knead with the dough hook for 5 minutes at low speed, then for 6 minutes at high speed. Add the olive oil and knead for another 2 minutes at high speed.

KNEADING BY HAND
Put the flour in a mixing bowl and make a large well in the center. Pour in half the water [1], then add the starter [2], fresh yeast, sugar, and salt. Mix well, then add the rest of the water little by little and mix together well [3]. Add the olive oil [4] and knead the dough until it no longer sticks to the sides of the mixing bowl [5]. Knead on the work surface until it becomes smooth and elastic.

Shape the dough into a ball, cover with a damp cloth, and leave to rise for 2 hours. Midway through the rise, deflate the dough by folding it in half. By the end of the rising time it will have increased in volume [6].

Dust the work surface. Divide the dough into two equal pieces. Use a rolling pin to roll each piece of dough out to the size of your baking sheets. The dough tends to shrink back as you roll it, so persist until it reaches the correct size.

Lift each piece of dough onto the baking sheets, lined with parchment (baking) paper. Prick all over with a fork, leaving a ½-inch (1-cm) border [7]. Cover with a damp cloth and leave to proof for 1 hour.

Spread each pizza with tomato sauce and top with slices or strips of ham. Sprinkle with oregano and Swiss cheese (Emmental) [8, 9].

Place a baking sheet on the bottom shelf of the oven and preheat to 460°F (235°C). Just before putting the pizzas in the oven, pour 50 g (scant ¼ cup) of water onto the preheated baking sheet. Bake the pizzas for 4 minutes, then lower the temperature to 425°F (220°C) and continue cooking for 11 minutes. Remove from the oven and brush the border of each pizza lightly with olive oil.

Oil-Enriched Breads

Oil-Enriched Breads

SWEET
PASTRIES
&
BREADS

PARIS BUNS

Makes 7 rolls,
each about 130 g

TIMINGS
- Mixing & kneading: 12 min
- First rising: 1 h
- Resting time: 15 min
- Proofing: 2 h
- Baking: 13–15 min

INGREDIENTS
- 500 g (4 cups) all-purpose (plain) flour, plus extra for dusting
- 230 g (scant 1 cup) milk
- 35 g (scant ¼ cup) superfine (caster) sugar
- 20 g (2 tablespoons) fresh baker's yeast, crumbled
- 10 g (2 teaspoons) salt
- 80 g (generous ⅓ cup) softened butter
- 1 lightly beaten egg, for glazing
- Nib sugar, for sprinkling

KNEADING IN A STAND MIXER
Put the flour, milk, sugar, fresh yeast, and salt in the bowl. Knead for 4 minutes at low speed, and then for 4 minutes at high speed. Add the butter and knead for another 4 minutes.

KNEADING BY HAND
Put the flour on a work surface or in a mixing bowl and make a large well in the center. Pour in half the milk, then add the sugar, fresh yeast, and salt. Mix well, then pour in the remaining milk and blend until all the flour has been incorporated. Add the butter and knead until the dough becomes smooth and elastic.

Shape into a ball and cover with a damp cloth. Leave to rise for 1 hour. The dough will have increased in volume by the end of the rising time [1].

Dust the work surface. Divide the dough into 7 equal pieces. Cover with a damp cloth and leave to rest for 15 minutes.

If you want to make round rolls, roll the dough pieces between the palms of your hands to shape them [2]. If you prefer a longer shape, use the palm of your hand to flatten each piece of dough gently into a rough oval. With the long side facing you, fold in a third towards the center and press along the edge with your fingertips. Swivel the dough 180 degrees. Fold one half on top of the other and seal the edges together with the heel of your hand. With lightly floured hands, roll the dough out to form batons, around 6 inches (15 cm) long [3].

Place the shaped rolls on a baking sheet lined with parchment (baking) paper, seams underneath. Brush with the lightly beaten egg. Leave to proof for 2 hours.

Place another baking sheet on the bottom shelf of the oven and preheat to 400°F (200°C). Glaze the rolls a second time [4]. Dip the blades of a pair of scissors into the beaten egg and decorate the rolls. For long ones, slide the scissors through the dough, making snips at even intervals [5]. For round ones, snip a cross in the top of the rolls.

Sprinkle the rolls with nib sugar. Just before putting the rolls in the oven, pour 50 g (scant ¼ cup) of water onto the preheated baking sheet. Bake for 13–15 minutes.

Remove from the oven and leave to cool on a wire rack.

Sweet Pastries & Breads

VIENNESE BREAD

Makes 5 rolls,
each about 190 g

TIMINGS
- Mixing & kneading: 15 min
- First rising: 1 h
- Resting time: 15 min
- Proofing: 1 h 30 min
- Baking: 15 min

INGREDIENTS
- 500 g (4 cups) all-purpose (plain) flour, plus extra for dusting
- 35 g (scant 3 tablespoons) sugar
- 10 g (2 teaspoons) salt
- 25 g (¼ cup) milk powder
- 225 g (scant 1 cup) water at 68°F (20°C)
- 75 g (⅓ cup) liquid sourdough starter (or 20 g [2½ tablespoons] dry sourdough starter)
- 15 g (1½ tablespoons) fresh baker's yeast, crumbled
- 75 g (⅓ cup) softened butter
- 1 egg, lightly beaten
- 200 g (generous 1 cup) chocolate chips (optional)

KNEADING IN A STAND MIXER
Put the flour, sugar, salt, milk powder, water, starter, and fresh yeast in the bowl. Knead for 5 minutes at low speed, then for 6 minutes at high speed [1]. Add the butter and knead for another 4 minutes. For the chocolate variation, add the chips at the end and mix in briefly.

KNEADING BY HAND
Put the flour, sugar, salt, and milk powder on a work surface or in a mixing bowl and make a large well in the center. Pour in half the water, then add the starter and fresh yeast. Mix well, then add the remaining water and blend until all the flour has been incorporated. Add the butter and knead the dough until it becomes smooth and elastic. For the chocolate variation, incorporate the chips at the end of the kneading process.

Shape into a ball and cover with a damp cloth. Leave to rise for 1 hour. The dough will have increased in volume by the end of the rising time.

Dust the work surface. Divide the dough into 5 equal pieces and shape them into balls. Cover with a damp cloth and leave to rest for 15 minutes.

Working with 1 piece of dough at a time, use the palm of your hand to flatten it gently into a rough oval. With the long side facing you, fold in a third towards the center and press along the edge with your fingertips. Swivel the dough 180 degrees. Fold in the other long edge so that it overlaps in the center and press with the heel of your hand. Fold one half on top of the other, and seal the edges together with the heel of your hand. With lightly floured hands, roll the dough out to form batons, around 6 inches (15 cm) long [2]. Shape the other batons the same way.

Place the shaped rolls on a baking sheet lined with parchment (baking) paper, seams underneath. Brush with the lightly beaten egg [3]. Refrigerate for 10 minutes, then glaze them again and score them in a "sausage" cut (see page 41) [4]. Leave to proof for 1 hour 30 minutes.

Place another baking sheet on the bottom shelf of the oven and preheat to 320°F (160°C).

Just before putting the loaves in the oven, pour 50 g (scant ¼ cup) of water onto the preheated baking sheet. Bake for 15 minutes.

Remove from the oven and leave to cool on a wire rack.

△ Try brushing the freshly baked rolls with melted butter.

Sweet Pastries & Breads

Sweet Pastries & Breads

SUGAR BREAD

Makes 3 loaves,
each about 270 g

TIMINGS

- Mixing & kneading: 10 min
- First rising: 1h
- Resting time: 1h
- Proofing: 1h 30 min
- Baking: 25 min

INGREDIENTS

- 500 g (4 cups) all-purpose (plain) flour
- 280 g (generous 1 cup) water at 68°F (20°C)
- 100 g (scant ½ cup) liquid sourdough starter (or 25 g [3 tablespoons] dry sourdough starter)
- 10 g (1 tablespoon) fresh baker's yeast, crumbled
- 10 g (2 teaspoons) salt
- 80 g (scant ½ cup) brown sugar
- Sunflower oil, for greasing

For the syrup:
- 50 g (¼ cup) turbinado (demerara) sugar
- 50 g (scant ¼ cup) water

Prepare the syrup the night before. Put the sugar and water in a saucepan and bring to a boil. Allow to cool, then pour into a pitcher and keep at room temperature overnight.

KNEADING IN A STAND MIXER

Put the flour, water, starter, fresh yeast, salt, and sugar in the bowl. Knead for 4 minutes at low speed, then for 6 minutes at high speed.

KNEADING BY HAND

Put the flour on a work surface or in a mixing bowl and make a large well in the center. Pour in half the water, then add the starter, yeast, salt, and sugar. Mix well, then add the remaining water and blend until all the flour has been incorporated. Knead the dough until it becomes smooth and elastic.

Shape into a ball and cover with a damp cloth. Leave to rise for 1 hour.

Divide the dough into 3 equal pieces and shape them into balls. Cover with a damp cloth and leave to rest for 1 hour.

Lightly oil the work surface. Turn out the dough balls, bringing their edges in to the center and pressing down gently. Turn them over and around on the work surface, pressing gently to form smooth, even-shaped balls. The oil will prevent the seams from opening. Cover with a damp cloth and leave to proof for 1 hour 30 minutes.

Place a baking sheet on the bottom shelf of the oven and preheat to 400°F (200°C). Put the loaves on another baking sheet lined with parchment (baking) paper, seams on top. Just before putting the loaves in the oven, pour 50 g (scant ¼ cup) of water onto the preheated baking sheet. Bake for 25 minutes.

Remove from the oven, brush with sugar syrup, and leave to cool on a wire rack.

△ Variation: Try flouring the work surface instead of oiling it. The loaves should then be baked seam side down. Just before putting them in the oven, score a cross on top of each.

Sweet Pastries & Breads

CLASSIC BRIOCHE

Makes 4 brioches,
each about 300 g

TIMINGS
- Mixing & kneading:
  15 min in the mixer,
  30 min by hand
- First rising: 2h
- Refrigeration: 1h
- Resting time: 30 min
- Proofing: 1h 30 min to 2h
- Baking: 25 min

INGREDIENTS
- 500 g (4 cups) all-purpose
  (plain) flour, plus extra
  for dusting
- 80 g (½ cup) superfine
  (caster) sugar
- 75 g (⅓ cup) liquid
  sourdough starter (or
  20 g dry sourdough
  starter)
- 20 g (2 tablespoons) fresh
  baker's yeast, crumbled
- 10 g (2 teaspoons) salt
- 6 eggs, plus 1 lightly
  beaten egg for glazing
- 250 g (generous 1 cup)
  softened butter, plus
  extra for greasing
- 5 g (1 teaspoon) vanilla
  extract
- Nib sugar, for sprinkling

You will need 4 brioche pans, each 6 ¼ inches (16 cm) in diameter.

KNEADING IN A STAND MIXER

Put the flour, sugar, starter, fresh yeast, salt, and eggs in the bowl. Knead for 5 minutes at low speed, then for 6 minutes at high speed [1]. Add the butter and vanilla and knead for another 4 minutes.

KNEADING BY HAND

Put the flour on a work surface or in a mixing bowl and make a large well in the center. Pour in the starter, then add the yeast, salt, sugar, and eggs. Blend until all the flour has been incorporated, then incorporate the butter and vanilla extract. Knead the dough for at least 30 minutes until it becomes smooth and elastic.

Shape the dough into a ball and cover it with a damp cloth. Leave to rise for 2 hours. It will have increased in volume by the end of the rising time [2]. Refrigerate it for 1 hour.

Dust the work surface. Divide the dough into 4 equal pieces. Shape into balls without working the dough too much. Cover with a damp cloth and leave to rest for 30 minutes.

Butter the brioche pans. Turn each piece of dough around between your hands, pressing down onto the work surface to shape them into well-rounded balls [3]. Place them in the brioche pans [4]. Leave to proof for 1 hour 30 minutes to 2 hours.

Place a baking sheet on the bottom shelf of the oven and preheat to 325°F (170°C). Glaze the brioches with lightly beaten egg [5]. Use scissors to score the tops crosswise [6, 7]. Sprinkle with nib sugar [8]. Just before putting the brioches in the oven, pour 50 g (scant ¼ cup) of water onto the preheated baking sheet. Bake for around 25 minutes. Remove from the oven, turn out the brioches, and leave them to cool on a wire rack.

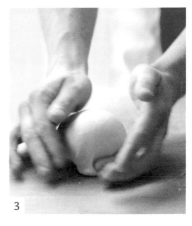

Sweet Pastries & Breads

MINI BRIOCHES

After chilling the dough, remove it from the fridge, divide it into 10 equal pieces, and shape them into balls. Leave to rest for 30 minutes. Working with a ball of dough at a time, use the palm of your hand to flatten each piece gently into a rough oval [1]. With the long side facing you, fold in a third towards the center and press with the palm of your hand [2]. Swivel the dough 180 degrees. Fold in the other long edge so that it overlaps in the center and press with the heel of your hand. Fold one half on top of the other, and seal the edges together with the heel of your hand. Roll gently [3], and then arrange them, side by side, on a baking sheet lined with parchment (baking) paper [4].

Cover with a damp cloth and leave to proof for 1 hour 30 minutes. Do not leave them any longer or they will fuse together into 1 piece. Glaze with beaten egg and sprinkle with nib sugar [5]. Bake for 15 minutes.

Sweet Pastries & Breads

BRIOCHE LOAF

Makes 1 loaf, about 1 kg

TIMINGS

- Mixing & kneading: 15 min
- First rising: 1 h
- Proofing: 1 h 30 min
- Baking: 30 min

INGREDIENTS

- 500 g (4 cups) all-purpose (plain) flour, plus extra for dusting
- 135 g (½ cup) water at 68°F (20°C)
- 3 eggs (135 g), plus 1 lightly beaten egg for glazing
- 75 g (⅓ cup) liquid sourdough starter (or 20 g dry sourdough starter)
- 20 g (2 tablespoons) fresh baker's yeast, crumbled
- 10 g (2 teaspoons) salt
- 25 g (¼ cup) milk powder
- 35 g (scant ¼ cup) sugar
- 75 g (⅓ cup) softened butter, plus extra for greasing
- 1 egg, lightly beaten

You will need a loaf pan around 16 × 4 inches (40 × 10 cm).

KNEADING IN A STAND MIXER

Put the flour, water, eggs, starter, fresh yeast, salt, milk powder, and sugar in the bowl. Knead for 5 minutes at low speed, then for 6 minutes at high speed. Add the butter and knead for another 4 minutes.

KNEADING BY HAND

Put the flour on a work surface or in a mixing bowl and make a large well in the center. Pour in half the water, then add the eggs, starter, fresh yeast, salt, milk powder, and sugar. Mix well, then add the rest of the water and blend until all the flour has been incorporated. Add the butter and knead the dough until it becomes smooth and elastic.

Shape the dough into a ball and cover it with a slightly damp cloth. Leave to rise for 1 hour. It will have increased in volume by the end of the rising time.

Dust the work surface. Butter the loaf pan. Divide the dough into 4 equal pieces. Fold each piece over on itself and roll between your hands to shape into a smooth ball. Place the balls in the loaf pan—they should fill it by a third without touching the sides.

Brush the brioche with lightly beaten egg. Leave to proof for 1 hour 30 minutes; if left any longer, the balls will spread too much in the pan.

Place a baking sheet on the bottom shelf of the oven and preheat to 350°F (180°C). Glaze the brioche again. Just before putting the brioche in the oven, pour 50 g (scant ¼ cup) of water onto the preheated baking sheet. Bake for around 30 minutes.

Remove the pan from the oven and turn out the brioche loaf. Leave to cool on a wire rack.

Sweet Pastries & Breads

RAISIN BENOITONS

Makes 12 slices,
each about 80 g

TIMINGS
- Mixing & kneading: 10 min
- First rising: 1h
- Proofing: 1h 30 min h
- Baking: 12-15 min

INGREDIENTS
- 300 g (2½ cups) all-purpose (plain) flour
- 200 g (2 cups) rye flour
- 380 g (1½ cups) water at 68°F (20°C)
- 75 g (⅓ cup) liquid sourdough starter (or 20 g [1½ tablespoons] dry sourdough starter)
- 10 g (1 tablespoon) fresh baker's yeast, crumbled
- 10 g (2 teaspoons) salt
- 300 g (2 cups) raisins
- 30 g (2 tablespoons) melted butter

KNEADING IN A STAND MIXER
Put the 2 flours, water, starter, fresh yeast, and salt in the bowl. Knead for 4 minutes at low speed, then for 6 minutes at high speed. Add the raisins and the butter and mix in at low speed.

KNEADING BY HAND
Put the 2 flours on a work surface or in a mixing bowl and make a large well in the center. Pour in half the water, then add the starter, fresh yeast, and salt. Mix well, then add the remaining water and blend until all the flour has been incorporated. Knead the dough until it becomes smooth and elastic. Add the raisins and butter at the end of the kneading time.

Shape the dough into a ball and cover it with a damp cloth. Leave to rise for 1 hour. It will have increased in volume by the end of the rising time.

Dust the work surface. Stretch the dough with your hands to make a flat piece around 16 inches (40 cm) long and ¾ inch (2 cm) thick [1]. Use a sharp knife to cut the dough in half [2], then slice each half into strips, each about 1¼-1½ inches (3-4 cm) wide and 8 inches (20 cm) long. Place the strips on a baking sheet lined with parchment (baking) paper [3], and cover with a damp cloth. Leave to proof for 1 hour 30 minutes.

Place another baking sheet on the bottom shelf of the oven and preheat to 425°F (220°C). Just before putting the benoitons in the oven, pour 50 g (scant ¼ cup) of water onto the preheated baking sheet. Bake for 12-15 minutes.

Remove from the oven, and leave to cool on a wire rack.

CROISSANTS

Makes 20 croissants,
each about 60 g

TIMINGS
- Mixing & kneading: 10 min
- Refrigeration: 4h
- Proofing: 2–2½ h
- Baking: 15 min

INGREDIENTS
- 500 g (4 cups) all-purpose (plain) flour, plus extra for dusting
- 220 g (scant 1 cup) water at 50°F (10°C)
- 50 g (3⅓ tablespoons) liquid sourdough starter (or 13 g [1½ tablespoons] dry sourdough starter)
- 20 g (2 tablespoons) fresh baker's yeast, crumbled
- 10 g (2 teaspoons) sea salt
- 70 g (⅓ cup) sugar
- 1 egg (50 g), plus 1 lightly beaten egg for glazing
- 25 g (2 tablespoons) softened butter, plus 250 g (generous 1 cup) chilled butter

KNEADING IN A STAND MIXER
Put the flour, water, starter, fresh yeast, salt, sugar, and 1 egg in the bowl. Knead for 5 minutes at low speed, then for 2 minutes at high speed. Add the softened butter and knead for another 3 minutes.

KNEADING BY HAND
Put the flour on a work surface or in a mixing bowl and make a large well in the center. Add the starter, fresh yeast, salt, sugar, egg, and the softened butter, then pour in half the water. Mix well, then add the remaining water and blend until all the flour has been incorporated. Knead the dough until it becomes smooth and elastic.

Shape the dough into a ball and put it in a bowl. Cover with a damp cloth and refrigerate for 1 hour.

Take the chilled butter out of the refrigerator and place it between 2 sheets of parchment (baking) paper. Soften, by lightly running a rolling pin over it [1], and gradually shape it into a rectangle.

Dust the work surface. Use a rolling pin to roll out the chilled dough to a 12 × 24-inch (30 × 60-cm) rectangle, ⅛ inch (3 mm) thick [2, 3]. From time to time, lift the dough off the work surface to check its size [4]. Roll out the butter to fit one half of the dough rectangle. Lift the butter onto the dough [5] and fold the other half of the dough over it [6]. Turn the dough 90 degrees, so that the opening is to the right [7].

Roll out the dough again to create a 12 × 36-inch (30 × 90-cm) rectangle [8, 9, 10]. Fold this rectangle into thirds [11], brushing off any excess flour as you go, if necessary [12, 13]. Wrap the dough in plastic wrap (clingfilm) [14], and make an indentation with your fingertip in one corner to indicate that you have made one turn [15]. Refrigerate for 1 hour.

Dust the work surface and take the dough out of the refrigerator. Repeat the previous step, rolling the dough to a 12 × 36-inch (30 × 90-cm) rectangle [16] and folding it in thirds [17]. Wrap in plastic wrap and make 2 indentations with your fingertips to indicate a second turn [18]. Refrigerate for 1 hour.

Again, roll out the dough again to create a 12 × 36-inch (30 × 90-cm) rectangle. Fold this rectangle into thirds. Wrap the dough in plastic wrap and make 3 fingertip indentations to indicate a third turn. Refrigerate for 1 hour.

Dust the work surface. Unwrap the dough and roll it out neatly to a long 13½ × 22-inch (34 × 55-cm) rectangle, 1/16–⅛ inch (2–3 mm) thick. Try to make it as straight and even as you can [19], trimming the edges to neaten, if need be. Fold the dough in half lengthwise [20], then unfold it and cut it in 2 along the length of the fold.

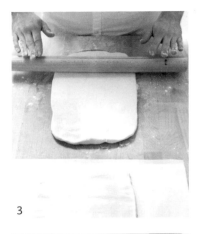

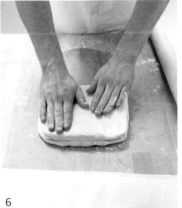

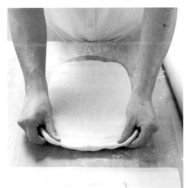

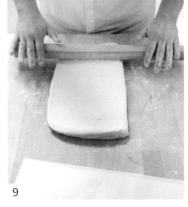

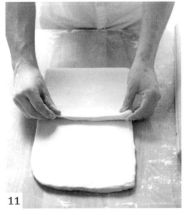

Sweet Pastries & Breads

Carefully lift 1 piece of dough to sit neatly on top of the other. Use a large knife to cut out triangles. Use a 4-inch (10-cm) dough cutter as a guide for the length of the triangle bases [21], with sides 7 inches (18 cm) long. Since the dough is in 2 layers, you will get 2 layers of triangles [22].

Roll up the croissants, working from the base to the point [23]. The point should ultimately rest underneath so that it does not unfold during baking. Throughout this process the dough triangles should remain well chilled; otherwise, it will be impossible to roll them. If they soften too much, return them to the refrigerator.

Arrange the croissants on wire racks covered with parchment (baking) paper. Leave to proof for 2–2½ hours. (You could place the racks in a cold oven, which then becomes a proofing chamber. Remove them before preheating the oven.)

Place a baking sheet on the bottom shelf of the oven and preheat to 325°F (170°C). Glaze the croissants with lightly beaten egg [24]. Just before putting the croissants in the oven, pour 50 g (scant ¼ cup) of water onto the preheated baking sheet. Bake for 15 minutes.

Remove from the oven, transfer the croissants to another wire rack, and leave to cool.

13

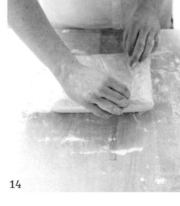

14

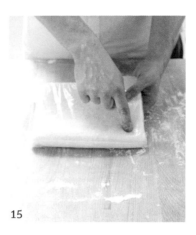

15

16

17

18

19

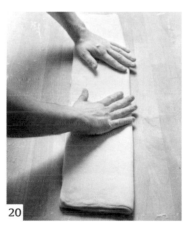

20

21

22

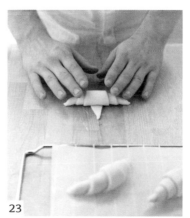

23

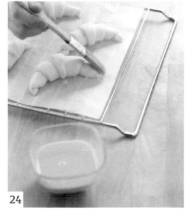

24

Sweet Pastries & Breads

PAIN AU CHOCOLAT

Makes 16 rolls,
each about 70 g

TIMINGS
• Mixing & kneading: 10 min
• Refrigeration: 4 h
• Proofing: 2 h
• Baking: 15 min

INGREDIENTS
• 500 g (4 cups) all-purpose
  (plain) flour
• 220 g (scant 1 cup) water
  at 50°F (10°C)
• 50 g (scant ¼ cup)
  liquid sourdough starter
  (or 13 g dry sourdough
  starter)
• 20 g (2 tablespoons) fresh
  baker's yeast, crumbled
• 10 g (2 teaspoons) salt
• 70 g (generous ⅓ cup)
  sugar
• 1 egg (50 g), plus 1 lightly
  beaten egg for glazing
• 25 g (1¾ tablespoons)
  softened butter, plus
  250 g (generous 1 cup)
  chilled butter
• 225 g (1 cup) dark
  chocolate, broken into
  squares

KNEADING IN A STAND MIXER
Put the flour, water, starter, fresh yeast, salt, sugar,
and egg in the bowl. Knead for 5 minutes at low speed, then
for 5 minutes at high speed. Add the softened butter around
3 minutes before the end of the kneading time.

KNEADING BY HAND
Put the flour on a work surface or in a mixing bowl and make
a large well in the center [1]. Add the starter, fresh yeast, salt,
sugar, egg, and the softened butter [2], then pour in half the
water [3]. Mix well, then add the remaining water [4] and
blend until all the flour has been incorporated [5, 6]. Knead
the dough by throwing it forcefully down onto the work surface
and then folding it [7, 8] until it becomes smooth and elastic.

Shape the dough into a ball [9]. Cover with a damp cloth
and refrigerate for 1 hour.

Take the chilled butter out of the refrigerator and place it
between 2 sheets of parchment (baking) paper. Soften by
lightly running a rolling pin over it, and gradually shape into
a rectangle.

Dust the work surface. Use a rolling pin to roll out the chilled
dough to a 12 × 24-inch (30 × 60-cm) rectangle, ⅛ inch
(3 mm) thick. From time to time, lift the dough off the work
surface to check its size. Roll out the butter to fit one half
of the dough rectangle. Lift the butter onto the dough and
fold the other half of the dough over it. Turn the dough 90
degrees, so that the opening is to the right.

Roll out the dough again to obtain a 12 × 36-inch (30 × 90-
cm) rectangle. Fold this rectangle into thirds, brushing off
any excess flour as you go, if necessary. Wrap the dough in
plastic wrap (clingfilm), and make an indentation with your
fingertip in one corner to indicate that you have made one
turn. Refrigerate for 1 hour.

Dust the work surface and take the dough out of the
refrigerator. Roll the dough out to a 12 × 36-inch (30 × 90-
cm) rectangle and folding it in thirds. Wrap in plastic wrap
and make 2 indentations with your fingertips to indicate a
second turn. Refrigerate for 1 hour.

Repeat this process for a final time. Roll the dough out
to a 12 × 36-inch (30 × 90-cm) rectangle and folding it in
thirds. Wrap the dough in plastic wrap and make 3 fingertip
indentations to indicate a third turn. Refrigerate for 1 hour.

Dust the work surface. Unwrap the dough and roll it out neatly
to a 16 x 24 inches (40 x 60cm) rectangle, ⅛ inch (3 mm)
thick [10]. Try to make it as straight and even as you can,
trimming the edges to neaten, if need be. Fold the dough
in half lengthwise, then unfold it and cut it in 2 along the
length of the fold.

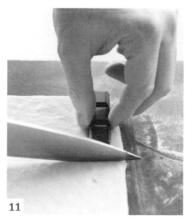

Sweet Pastries & Breads

Arrange squares of chocolate along the long edge of each piece of dough. Use a large knife to cut each piece of dough into rectangles, using 3 squares of chocolate as a guide for the width [11]. Make sure that each rectangle is slightly wider than the chocolate so it doesn't protrude from the ends when you roll it up. You should achieve a total of 16 rectangles, each about 6 by 4 inches (15 x 10 cm).

Roll up each pain au chocolat, making about 3 turns. The seam should ultimately rest underneath [12] so that it does not unfold during baking. Throughout this process the dough pieces should remain well chilled; otherwise, it will be impossible to roll them. If they soften too much, return them to the refrigerator.

Arrange the pains au chocolat on baking sheets lined with parchment (baking) paper. Leave to proof for 2 hours. (You could place the sheets in a cold oven, which then becomes a proofing chamber. Remove them before preheating the oven.)

Place another baking sheet on the bottom shelf of the oven and preheat to 325°F (170°C). Glaze the pains au chocolat with lightly beaten egg. Just before putting them in the oven, pour 50 g (scant ¼ cup) of water onto the preheated baking sheet. Bake for 15 minutes.

Remove from the oven and leave to cool on a wire rack.

VANILLA ROLLS

Makes 16 rolls,
each about 60 g

TIMINGS
- Mixing & kneading: 12 min
- First rising: 1h 10 min
- Resting: 30 min
- Proofing: 1h 20 min
- Baking: 15 min

INGREDIENTS
- 500 g (4 cups) all-purpose (plain) flour, plus extra for dusting
- 280 g (generous 1 cup) water at 68°F (20°C)
- 100 g (scant ½ cup) liquid sourdough starter (or 25 g [3 tablespoons] dry sourdough starter)
- 80 g (scant ½ cup) turbinado [demerara] sugar
- 30 g (2 tablespoons) canola (rapeseed) oil
- 15 g (4½ teaspoons) fresh baker's yeast, crumbled
- 4 vanilla beans, split and scraped
- 10 g (2 teaspoons) salt

KNEADING IN A STAND MIXER
Put the flour, water, starter, sugar, fresh yeast, oil, and salt in the bowl. Knead for 4 minutes at low speed, then for 8 minutes at high speed. Add the vanilla at the end of the kneading time.

KNEADING BY HAND
Put the flour on a work surface or in a mixing bowl and make a large well in the center. Pour in half the water, then add the starter, sugar, oil, salt, and vanilla. Mix well, then add the rest of the water and blend until all the flour has been incorporated. Knead the dough until it becomes smooth and elastic.

Shape the dough into a ball and cover with a damp cloth. Leave to rise for 1 hour 10 minutes.

Dust the work surface. Divide the dough into 16 equal pieces and shape them into balls. Cover with a damp cloth and leave to rest for 30 minutes.

Shape 8 of the dough pieces into little balls by rolling them between the palms of your hands. Make the remaining 8 into batons. Use the palm of your hand to flatten each piece of dough gently into a rough oval. With the long side facing you, fold in a third towards the center and press along the edge with your fingertips. Swivel the dough 180 degrees. Fold one half on top of the other, and seal the edges together with the heel of your hand. With lightly floured hands, roll the dough out to form a baton, around 4–4½ inches (10–12 cm) long. Shape the remaining rolls the same way.

Place the shaped rolls on a baking sheet lined with parchment (baking) paper, seams underneath. Leave to proof for 1 hour 20 minutes.

Place another baking sheet on the bottom shelf of the oven and preheat to 400°F (200°C). Score the round rolls in a star pattern and the long batons with a "sausage" cut (see page 41), or simply make 2–4 long slashes.

Just before putting the loaves in the oven, pour 50 g (scant ¼ cup) of water onto the preheated baking sheet. Bake for 15 minutes.

Remove from the oven and leave to cool on a wire rack.

Sweet Pastries & Breads

PULLMAN LOAF

Makes 2 loaves,
each about 500 g

TIMINGS
• Mixing & kneading: 15 min
• First rising: 1 h
• Resting: 15 min
• Proofing: 1 h 30 min
• Baking: 30–40 min

INGREDIENTS
• 500 g (4 cups) all-purpose
  (plain) flour, plus extra
  for dusting
• 280 g (generous 1 cup)
  water at 68°F (20°C)
• 75 g (⅓ cup) liquid
  sourdough starter (or
  20 g [2½ tablespoons]
  dry sourdough starter)
• 20 g (2 tablespoons) fresh
  baker's yeast, crumbled
• 10 g (2 teaspoons) salt
• 10 g (2 tablespoons)
  milk powder
• 40 g (scant ¼ cup) sugar
• 40 g (scant 3 tablespoons)
  softened butter, plus
  extra for greasing
• 20 g (4 teaspoons)
  crème fraîche
• 1 egg, lightly beaten

You will need 2 loaf pans, each about 6½ × 3 × 3 inches
(17 × 7.5 × 7.5 cm).

KNEADING IN A STAND MIXER
Put the flour, water, starter, fresh yeast, salt, milk powder,
and sugar in the bowl. Knead for 5 minutes at low speed,
then for 6 minutes at high speed. Add the butter [1] and the
crème fraîche and knead for another 4 minutes. Knead well
to obtain a smooth dough.

KNEADING BY HAND
Put the flour on a work surface or in a mixing bowl and make
a large well in the center. Pour in half the water, then add the
starter, fresh yeast, salt, milk powder, and sugar. Mix well,
then add the rest of the water and blend until all the flour
has been incorporated. Add the butter and the crème fraîche
and knead until the dough becomes smooth and elastic.

Shape the dough into a ball and cover with a damp cloth.
Leave to rise for 1 hour. By the end of the rising time it will
have increased in volume.

Dust the work surface. Divide the dough into 4 equal pieces
and shape them into balls without working the dough too
much [2]. Cover with a damp cloth and leave to rest for
15 minutes.

Butter the molds [3]. Place 2 pieces of dough in each loaf
pan; they should fill them by two-thirds.

Brush with the lightly beaten egg. Leave to proof for
1 hour 30 minutes. By the end of the proofing time the dough
will have expanded in each pan to form 1 loaf.

Place a baking sheet on the bottom shelf of the oven
and preheat to 325°F (170°C). Glaze the loaves a second time.
Just before putting the loaves in the oven, pour 50 g
(scant ¼ cup) of water onto the preheated baking sheet.
Bake for 30–40 minutes.

Remove the loaves from the oven. Turn them out and leave
to cool on a wire rack.

1

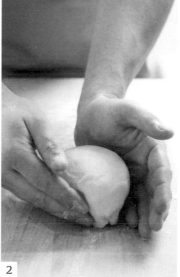
2

3

Sweet Pastries & Breads

PISTACHIO LOAF

Follow the recipe above, adding 40 g (2 ½ tablespoons) of pistachio paste at the end of the kneading time. Shape the dough into balls. Turn each piece around on the work surface, bring the edges in to the center, and press down lightly. Turn them over and around again, pressing down all the while. Continue with the proofing and baking as in the main recipe.

After baking, turn the loaves out and cool them on a wire rack. Brush them with sugar syrup (see page 240) and sprinkle with finely chopped pistachios. Dust with confectioners' (icing) sugar, using a spatula angled across the surface of the loaf to achieve a striped pattern.

Sweet Pastries & Breads

PAIN AUX RAISINS

Makes 18 rolls,
each about 85 g

TIMINGS
- Mixing & kneading: 10 min
- Refrigeration: 4h
- Proofing: 2h
- Baking: 15 min

INGREDIENTS
- 500 g (4 cups) all-purpose (plain) flour
- 220 g (scant 1 cup) water at 50°F (10°C)
- 50 g (scant ¼ cup) liquid sourdough starter (or 13 g [1½ tablespoons] dry sourdough starter)
- 20 g (2 tablespoons) fresh baker's yeast, crumbled
- 10 g (2 teaspoons) salt
- 70 g (generous ⅓ cup) sugar
- 1 egg (50 g), plus 1 lightly beaten egg, for glazing
- 25 g (1¾ tablespoons) softened butter, plus 250 g (generous 1 cup) chilled butter
- 150 g (1 cup) golden raisins (sultanas)

For the pastry cream:
- 1 vanilla bean, split and scraped
- 500 g (generous 2 cups) milk
- 2 eggs
- 120 g (scant ⅔ cup) sugar
- 50 g (scant ½ cup) cornstarch (cornflour)

For the sugar syrup:
- 100 g (½ cup) sugar
- 100 g (scant ½ cup) water

Make the pastry cream. Add the milk and vanilla to a saucepan and bring to a boil. Whisk the eggs and sugar in a mixing bowl until pale and creamy. Add the cornstarch (cornflour) and whisk until evenly blended. Pour a third of the hot milk onto the eggs and whisk in well. Tip this mixture back into the saucepan and cook over a low heat, whisking, until it thickens. Make sure you whisk right down to the bottom of the saucepan as well as around the sides. Remove from the heat as soon as the cream starts to bubble. Pour into a mixing bowl and leave to cool.

KNEADING IN A STAND MIXER
Put the flour, water, starter, fresh yeast, salt, sugar, and 1 egg into the bowl. Knead for 5 minutes at low speed, then for 2 minutes at high speed. Add the softened butter and knead for another 3 minutes on high speed, and mix in well.

KNEADING BY HAND
Put the flour on a work surface or in a mixing bowl and make a large well in the center. Add half the water, then add the starter, fresh yeast, salt, sugar, 1 egg, and softened butter. Mix well, then add the rest of the water and blend until all the flour has been incorporated. Knead the dough until it becomes smooth and elastic.

Shape into a ball and cover with a damp cloth. Refrigerate for 1 hour.

Take the chilled butter out of the refrigerator and place it between 2 sheets of parchment (baking) paper. Soften, by lightly running a rolling pin over the surface, and gradually shape it into a rectangle.

Dust the work surface. Use a rolling pin to roll out the chilled dough to a 12 × 23 inch (30 × 60 cm) rectangle, ⅛ inch (3 mm) thick. From time to time, lift the dough off the work surface to check its size. Roll out the butter to fit one half of the dough rectangle. Lift the butter onto the dough and fold the other half of the dough over it. Turn the dough 90 degrees, so that the opening is to the right.

Roll out the dough again to obtain a rectangle one-third longer than the previous one. Fold this rectangle into thirds, brushing off any excess flour as you go, if necessary. Wrap the dough in plastic wrap (clingfilm), and make an indentation with your fingertip in one corner to indicate that you have made one turn. Refrigerate for 1 hour.

Dust the work surface and take the dough out of the refrigerator. Repeat the previous step, rolling the dough and folding it in thirds. Wrap in plastic wrap and make 2 indentations with your fingertips to indicate a second turn. Refrigerate for 1 hour.

Sweet Pastries & Breads

Repeat this process for a final time. Wrap the dough in plastic wrap and make 3 fingertip indentations to indicate a third turn. Refrigerate for 1 hour.

Dust the work surface. Unwrap the dough and roll it out neatly to a rectangle, ⅛ inch (3 mm) thick. It should be around 16 inches (40 cm) long by 12 inches (30 cm) wide. Try to make it as straight and even as you can.

Whisk the pastry cream to loosen it (either by hand or in a stand mixer) [1, 2]. Use a spatula to spread it evenly over the dough [3]. Scatter the golden raisins (sultanas) over the entire surface [4].

Roll up the dough lengthwise into a long log [5], finishing with the seam underneath [6]. Cut into 18 slices, each ⅝ inch (1.5 cm) thick [7], and place them on wire racks (or baking sheets) covered with parchment (baking) paper. Glaze them with the lightly beaten egg [8]. Leave to proof for 2 hours. (You could place the racks in a cold oven, which then becomes a proofing chamber. Remove them before preheating the oven.)

While the dough is proofing, prepare the sugar syrup by bringing the water and sugar to a boil. Remove from the heat and leave to cool.

Place another baking sheet on the bottom shelf of the oven and preheat to 325°F (170°C). Glaze the pain aux raisins with eggs again. Just before putting them in the oven, pour 50 g (scant ¼ cup) of water onto the preheated baking sheet. Bake for 15 minutes.

Remove the pain aux raisins from the oven and leave to cool on a wire rack. Use a brush to glaze them with sugar syrup [9].

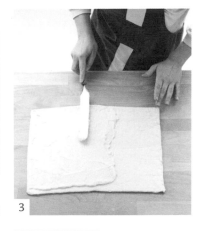

267   Sweet Pastries & Breads

BREAD
ROLLS

POPPY SEED ROLLS

Makes 17 rolls,
each about 60 g

TIMINGS

- Mixing & kneading: 10 min
- First rising: 1 h 30 min
- Resting: 15 min
- Proofing: 1 h 30 min
- Baking: 24 min

INGREDIENTS

- 100 g (scant ⅔ cup)
  poppy seeds,
  plus extra for topping
- 500 g (scant 4¼ cups)
  all-purpose (plain) flour,
  plus extra for dusting
- 320 g (1¼ cups) water
  at 68°F (20°C), plus 30 g
  (2 tablespoons)
  for steeping the seeds
- 100 g (scant ½ cup)
  liquid sourdough starter
  (or 25 g [3 tablespoons]
  dry sourdough starter)
- 5 g (1½ teaspoons)
  fresh baker's yeast
- 10 g (1¾ teaspoons) salt

Preheat the oven to 475°F (240°C). Spread out the weighed poppy seeds [1] on a baking sheet lined with parchment (baking) paper and toast for 10 minutes. Tip them immediately into a bowl with the 30 g (2 tablespoons) water and leave to steep for a few minutes. Set aside.

KNEADING IN A STAND MIXER

Put the flour, water, starter, fresh yeast, and salt in the bowl. Knead with the dough hook for 4 minutes at low speed, then 6 minutes at high speed. Towards the end of the kneading time, add the toasted poppy seeds, and mix in gently.

KNEADING BY HAND

Put the flour on a work surface or in a mixing bowl and make a large well in the center. Pour in half the water, then add the starter, fresh yeast, and salt. Mix well, then add the remaining water and the toasted poppy seeds and mix until all the flour has been incorporated. Knead the dough until it becomes smooth and elastic.

Shape into a ball and cover with a damp cloth and leave to rise for 1 hour 30 minutes. It will have increased in volume by the end of the rising time.

Dust the work surface. Divide the dough into 17 equal pieces and shape into balls. Cover with a damp cloth and leave to rest for 15 minutes.

Cover a plate with extra poppy seeds. Shape the dough into little balls by rolling them between the palms of your hands, or into batons [2]. (To form the batons, follow the method on page 234). Brush or spray the rolls lightly with water and roll them in the poppy seeds to coat evenly all over.

Arrange the rolls on baking sheets lined with parchment (baking) paper, seams underneath. Cover with a damp cloth and leave to proof for 1 hour 30 minutes.

Place another baking sheet on the bottom shelf of the oven and preheat to 450°F (230°C).

Score the rolls with your favorite design [3] using a bread lame or scissors. Just before putting the rolls in the oven, pour 50 g (scant ¼ cup) of water onto the preheated baking sheet. Bake for 14 minutes.

Remove from the oven and leave to cool on a wire rack.

271

BREAD ROLLS WITH LARDONS & PECANS

Makes 20 rolls,
each about 60 g

TIMINGS
- Mixing & kneading: 10 min
- First rising: 1 h 30 min
- Resting: 30 min
- Proofing: 1 h 30 min
- Baking: 14 min

INGREDIENTS
- 200 g smoked bacon
  (or lardons) (20% of the
  dough's weight)
- 100 g (2/3 cup) pecan halves
  (10% of the dough's weight)
- 500 g (scant 4 1/4 cups)
  all-purpose (plain) flour,
  plus extra for dusting
- 310 g (scant 1 1/4 cups)
  water at 68°F (20°C)
- 100 g (scant 1/2 cup)
  liquid sourdough starter
  (or 25 g [3 tablespoons]
  dry sourdough starter)
- 5 g (1 1/2 teaspoons)
  fresh baker's yeast
- 10 g (1 3/4 teaspoons) salt

Cut the bacon into matchsticks [1]. Brown in a frying pan over medium heat. Drain in a sieve [2]. Mix with the pecans [3].

KNEADING IN A STAND MIXER
Put the flour, water, starter, fresh yeast, and salt in the bowl. Knead with the dough hook for 4 minutes at low speed, then 6 minutes at high speed. Towards the end of the kneading time add the lardons and pecans and mix in gently.

KNEADING BY HAND
Put the flour on a work surface or in a mixing bowl and make a large well in the center. Pour in half the water, then add the starter, fresh yeast, and salt. Mix well, then add the remaining water and knead until all the flour has been incorporated. Knead the dough until smooth and elastic. Add the lardons and pecans towards the end of the kneading.

Shape into a ball and cover with a damp cloth. Leave to rise for 1 hour 30 minutes. It will have increased in volume by the end of the rising time.

Divide the dough into 20 equal pieces and shape into balls [3]. Cover with a damp cloth and leave to rest for 30 minutes.

Working with one ball of dough at a time, use the palm of your hand to flatten it gently [4]. Fold in a third towards the center [5] and press with your fingertips [6]. Swivel the dough 180 degrees. Fold in the other edge so that it overlaps in the center and press again. Fold one half on top of the other and seal the edges together with the heel of your hand [7]. With lightly floured hands, roll the dough out to form a plump oval [8]. Shape the other rolls the same way. You can also shape the dough into round rolls (see page 274).

Place the rolls on baking sheets lined with parchment (baking) paper, seams underneath. Cover with a damp cloth and leave to proof for 1 hour 30 minutes.

Place another baking sheet on the bottom shelf of the oven and preheat to 450°F (230°C). Score the rolls with your favorite design using a bread lame [9]. Just before putting the loaves in the oven, pour 50 g (scant 1/4 cup) of water onto the preheated baking sheet. Bake for 14 minutes.

Remove from the oven and leave to cool on a wire rack.

273   Bread Rolls

Bread Rolls with Lardons & Pecans   274

Bread Rolls

PISTOLETS

Makes 12 pistolets,
each about 75 g

TIMINGS
- Mixing & kneading: 10 min
- First rising: 1h 30 min
- Resting: 30 min
- Proofing: 1h 30 min
- Baking: 14 min

INGREDIENTS
- 500 g (scant 4¼ cups) all-purpose (plain) flour, plus extra for dusting
- 310 g (scant 1¼ cups) water at 68°F (20°C)
- 100 g (scant ½ cup) liquid sourdough starter (or 25 g [3 tablespoons] dry sourdough starter)
- 10 g (1¾ teaspoons) salt
- 3 g (1 teaspoon) fresh baker's yeast

KNEADING IN A STAND MIXER
Put the flour, water, starter, salt, and fresh yeast in the bowl. Knead with the dough hook for 4 minutes at low speed, then 6 minutes at high speed.

KNEADING BY HAND
Put the flour on a work surface or in a mixing bowl and make a large well in the center. Add half the water, then add the starter, salt, and fresh yeast. Mix well, then add the remaining water and mix until all the flour has been incorporated. Knead the dough until it becomes smooth and elastic.

Shape the dough into a ball and cover with a damp cloth. Leave to rise for 1 hour 30 minutes. It will have increased in volume by the end of the rising time.

Dust the work surface. Divide the dough into 12 equal pieces and roll them into balls [1]. Leave to rest under a damp cloth for 30 minutes.

Working with one ball of dough at a time, use the palm of your hand to flatten it gently. Fold in a third towards the center [2] and press with your fingertips. Swivel the dough 180 degrees. Fold in the other edge so that it overlaps in the center and press again. Fold one half on top of the other and seal the edges together with the heel of your hand. With lightly floured hands, roll the dough out to form a plump oval [3]. Dust with flour [4]. Use a mini rolling pin to press into the roll along its length [5], then bring the edges together [6]. Shape the other pistolets the same way.

Arrange the pistolets on baking sheets lined with parchment (baking) paper. Cover with a damp cloth and leave to proof for 1 hour 30 minutes.

Place another baking sheet on the bottom shelf of the oven and preheat to 450°F (230°C). Just before putting the pistolets in the oven, pour 50 g (scant ¼ cup) of water onto the preheated baking sheet. Bake for 14 minutes.

Remove from the oven and leave to cool on a wire rack.

Bread Rolls

KAMUT®
&
SEAWEED
ROLLS

Makes 17 rolls,
each about 50–60 g

TIMINGS
• Mixing & kneading: 8 min
• Resting: 30 min
• Proofing: 2 h
• Baking: 14 min

INGREDIENTS
• 90 g dried seaweed
• 300 g (2 1/2 cups)
  whole-grain organic
  Kamut® flour
• 200 g (1 2/3 cups)
  all-purpose (plain) flour,
  plus extra for dusting
• 300 g (1 1/4 cups) water
  at 68°F (20°C)
• 150 g (2/3 cup) liquid
  sourdough starter
  (or 30 g [1 1/2 tablespoons]
  dry sourdough starter)
• 10 g (1 3/4 teaspoons) salt
• 2 g (2/3 teaspoon)
  fresh baker's yeast

Rehydrate the seaweed in a bowl of cold water.

KNEADING IN A STAND MIXER
Put the two flours, water, starter, salt, and fresh yeast
in the bowl. Knead with the dough hook for 4 minutes at low
speed, then 4 minutes at high speed. Toward the end of the
kneading time add the drained seaweed and mix in gently.

KNEADING BY HAND
Put the two flours on a work surface or in a mixing bowl and
make a large well in the center. Pour in half the water, then
add the starter, salt, and fresh yeast. Mix well, then add
the remaining water and the drained seaweed and mix until
all the flour has been incorporated. Knead the dough until it
becomes smooth and elastic.

Shape into a ball and cover with a damp cloth. Leave to rise
for 30 minutes. It will have increased in volume by the end
of the rising time.

Dust the work surface. Use your hands to flatten the dough
out to a thickness of around 3/4 inches (2 cm). Use a 2 1/2-inch
(6-cm) bread lame, to cut out squares, each around 50–60 g.

Place the dough squares on baking sheets lined with parchment
(baking) paper. Cover with a damp cloth and leave to proof
for 2 hours.

Place another baking sheet on the bottom shelf of the oven
and preheat to 435°F (225°C). Lightly dust the rolls with the
Kamut® flour and score with a lame into a cross, a diagonal,
or a leaf shape. Just before putting the loaves in the oven,
pour 50 g (scant 1/4 cup) of water onto the preheated baking
sheet. Bake for 14 minutes.

Remove from the oven and leave to cool on a wire rack.

Bread Rolls

HAZELNUT & CHOCOLATE ROLLS

Makes 10 rolls,
each about 120 g

TIMINGS
- Mixing & kneading: 14 min
- First rising: 1 h 30 min
- Resting: 15 min
- Refrigeration: 10 min
- Proofing: 1 h 15 min
- Baking: 15 min

INGREDIENTS
- 90 g (scant 2/3 cup)
  hazelnuts
  (10% of the dough's weight)
- 90 g dark chocolate
  (10% of the dough's weight)
- 500 g (scant 4 1/4 cups)
  all-purpose (plain) flour
- 250 g (1 cup) water
  at 68°F (20°C)
- 100 g (scant 1/2 cup)
  liquid sourdough starter
  (or 25 g [3 tablespoons]
  dry sourdough starter)
- 7 g (2 1/3 teaspoons)
  fresh baker's yeast
- 10 g (1 3/4 teaspoons) salt
- 25 g (1/4 cup) milk powder
- 35 g (scant 1/4 cup) sugar
- 75 g (1/3 cup)
  softened butter
- 1 lightly beaten egg,
  for glazing the rolls

Preheat the oven to 500°F (250°C). Crush the hazelnuts roughly, then spread them out in a baking pan and toast for 10 minutes [1, 2]. Leave to cool. Roughly chop the chocolate [3] and mix with the hazelnuts [4].

KNEADING IN A STAND MIXER
Put the flour, water, starter, fresh yeast, salt, milk powder, and sugar in the bowl. Knead with the dough hook for 4 minutes at low speed, then 7 minutes at high speed. Add the butter and knead for another 3 minutes [5]. Add the hazelnuts and chocolate [6] and mix in gently.

KNEADING BY HAND
Put the flour on a work surface or in a mixing bowl and make a large well in the center. Pour in half the water, then add the starter, fresh yeast, salt, milk powder, and the sugar. Mix well, then add the remaining water and knead until all the flour has been incorporated. Add the butter, then knead until the dough becomes smooth and elastic. Add the hazelnuts and the chocolate toward the end of the kneading process.

Shape into a ball on a lightly floured work surface. Cover with a damp cloth and leave to rise for 1 hour 30 minutes. It will have increased in volume by the end of the rising time [7].

Divide the dough into 10 equal pieces [8] and shape into balls. Cover with a damp cloth and leave to rest for 15 minutes.

Working with one ball of dough at a time, use the palm of your hand to flatten it gently. Fold in a third towards the center and press with your fingertips. Swivel the dough 180 degrees. Fold in the other edge so that it overlaps in the center and press again. Fold one half on top of the other and seal the edges together with the heel of your hand [9]. With lightly floured hands, roll the dough out to around 6 inches (15 cm) [10]. Shape the other rolls the same way.

Arrange the rolls on wire racks or baking sheets lined with parchment (baking) paper, seams underneath. Use a brush to glaze them with the lightly beaten egg [11]. Refrigerate for 10 minutes. Glaze the rolls a second time and score them in a "sausage" cut (see page 41) [12]. Cover with a damp cloth and leave to proof for 1 hour 15 minutes.

Place another baking sheet on the bottom shelf of the oven and preheat to 400°F (200°C). Just before putting the loaves in the oven, pour 50 g (scant 1/4 cup) of water onto the preheated baking sheet. Bake for 15 minutes.

Remove from the oven and leave to cool on a wire rack.

  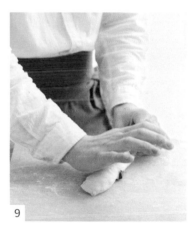

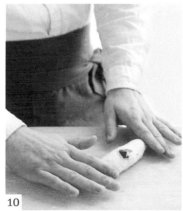  

Bread Rolls

Hazelnut & Chocolate Rolls   282

Bread Rolls

WALNUT & RAISIN ROLLS

Makes 6 rolls,
each about 190 g

TIMINGS
- Mixing & kneading: 8 min
- First rising: 1 h
- Resting: 15 min
- Proofing: 1 h 30 min
- Baking: 15-18 min

INGREDIENTS
- 250 g (2 cups) all-purpose (plain) flour
- 250 g (1 2/3 cups) light rye flour
- 350 g (1 1/2 cups) water at 68°F (20°C)
- 100 g (scant 1/2 cup) liquid sourdough starter (or 25 g [3 tablespoons] dry sourdough starter)
- 3 g (1 teaspoon) fresh baker's yeast
- 10 g (1 3/4 teaspoons) salt
- 100 g (1 cup) walnut halves
- 100 g (2/3 cup) raisins

Slice the walnuts in half and mix them with the raisins.

KNEADING IN A STAND MIXER
Put the two flours, the water, starter, fresh yeast, and salt in the bowl. Knead with the dough hook for 6 minutes at low speed, then 2 minutes at high speed. Add the walnuts and raisins and mix in gently.

KNEADING BY HAND
Put the two flours on the work surface or in a mixing bowl and make a large well in the center. Pour in half the water, then add the starter, fresh yeast, and salt. Mix well, then add the remaining water and mix until all the flour has been incorporated. Knead the dough until it becomes smooth and elastic. Incorporate the walnuts and raisins at the end of the kneading time.

Shape into a ball [14]. Cover with a damp cloth and leave to rise for 1 hour. It will have increased in volume by the end of the rising time.

Dust the work surface. Divide the dough into 6 equal pieces and shape into balls. Cover with a damp cloth and leave to rest for 15 minutes.

Roll out the balls to mini baguettes, around 6 inches (15 cm) long [2].

Arrange the rolls on baking sheets lined with parchment (baking) paper, seams underneath [3]. Cover with a damp cloth and leave to proof for 1 hour 30 minutes.

Place another baking sheet on the bottom shelf of the oven and preheat to 450°F (230°C). Just before putting the rolls in the oven, pour 50 g (scant 1/4 cup) of water onto the preheated baking sheet. Bake for 15-18 minutes.

Remove from the oven and leave to cool on a wire rack.

Bread Rolls

BREAD-STICKS

Makes 16 breadsticks, each about 50 g

TIMINGS

• Mixing & kneading: 10 min
• First rising: 1 h
• Proofing: 45 min
• Baking: 9 min

INGREDIENTS

• 500 g (scant 4 1/4 cups) all-purpose (plain) flour, plus extra for dusting
• 225 g (scant 1 cup) water at 68°F (20°C)
• 50 g liquid sourdough starter (or 12 g [1 1/2 tablespoons] dry sourdough starter)
• 10 g (1 tablespoon) fresh baker's yeast
• 10 g (1 3/4 teaspoons) salt
• 75 g (1/3 cup) extra-virgin olive oil

KNEADING IN A STAND MIXER

Put the flour, water, starter, fresh yeast, and salt in the bowl. Knead with the dough hook for 4 minutes at low speed, then 4 minutes at high speed. Add the oil and knead for another 2 minutes.

KNEADING BY HAND

Put the flour on a work surface or in a mixing bowl and make a large well in the center. Pour in half the water, then add the starter, fresh yeast, and salt. Mix well, then add the remaining water and the oil. Mix until all the flour has been incorporated. Knead the dough until smooth and elastic.

Shape into a ball and cover with a damp cloth. Leave to rise for 1 hour. Midway through the rise, deflate the dough by folding it in half. The dough will have increased in volume by the end of the rising time.

Dust the work surface. Gently flatten the dough with your hands [1], then roll it out to a rectangle about 16 inches (40 cm) long and 1/2 inch (1 cm) thick [2]. Trim the edges with a knife to neaten them [3]. Cut the dough in half to create two 8-inch (20-cm) pieces. Cut one portion into 1/2 inch (1 cm) strips and the other portion into 3/4 inch (2 cm) strips [4].

Use a bread lame to split the wider strips in half lengthwise [5], leaving them attached at each end. Insert a finger into the opening at each end and twist [6]. Roll all the twisted strips and all the plain strips gently on the work surface to lengthen them. They should be around 12 inches (30 cm) long.

Carefully lift the breadsticks onto baking sheets lined with parchment (baking) paper [7]. Leave to proof for 45 minutes.

Place another baking sheet on the bottom shelf of the oven and preheat to 450°F (230°C). Just before putting the breadsticks in the oven, pour 50 g (scant 1/4 cup) of water onto the preheated baking sheet. Bake for 9 minutes.

Remove from the oven and leave to cool on a wire rack.

△ Breadsticks—or grissini—lend themselves to endless variations. You can add chopped olives, sun-dried tomatoes, herbs (such as rosemary or thyme), or spices to the dough. The dough can also be colored with cuttlefish or squid ink for stylish black breadsticks. The ingredients should be added to the dough at the end of the kneading time. For sesame or poppy-seed breadsticks, after shaping them, roll in a tray of the seeds to coat evenly.

Bread Rolls

Breadsticks

Bread Rolls

APPENDIX

BULK CONVERSIONS

The recipes in the previous chapters are intended for home baking on a standard scale; however, the following charts provide measurements to make larger quantities on the basis of 1 kg flour. Measurements are provided as weights to ensure accuracy.

Bread	Base Temp.	Oven Temp.	Rising time (1st and 2nd rise) / Baking time	Ingredients	Dough weight per loaf	Comments
TRADITIONAL LOAVES						
BOULE (p. 45)	132.8°F (56°C)	480°F (250°C)	• 1 hr 30 mins and 1 hr 30 mins • 24 mins	• 1 kg all-purpose (plain) flour • 660 g water • 200 g liquid sourdough starter • 4 g fresh baker's yeast • 20 g salt	920 g	
BATARD (p. 52)	132.8°F (56°C)	480°F (250°C)	• 1 hr 30 mins and 1 hr 30 mins • 20 mins	• 1 kg all-purpose (plain) flour • 650 g water • 200 g liquid sourdough starter • 4 g fresh baker's yeast • 20 g salt	300 g	
BAGUETTE (p. 54)	136.4°F (58°C)	480°F (250°C)	• 1st resting 1 hr then 1 hr 30 mins and 1 hr 20 mins • 20 mins (25 mins in damp weather conditions)	• 1 kg all-purpose (plain) flour • 650 g water • 200 g liquid sourdough starter • 5 g fresh baker's yeast • 20 g salt	300 g	Bassinage* water added 3 mins before end of kneading.
POLKA BREAD (p. 56)	132.8°F (56°C)	480°F (250°C)	• 1st resting 1 hr then 1 hr 30 mins and 1 hr 30 mins • 25 mins	• 1 kg all-purpose (plain) flour • 650 g water • 200 g liquid sourdough starter • 5 g fresh baker's yeast • 20 g salt	460 g	Bassinage* water added 3 mins before end of kneading.
FANCY LOAVES: EPI, FICELLE & BRAIDED (p. 58)	132.8°F (56°C)	480°F (250°C)	• 1st resting 1 hr then 1 hr 30 mins and 1 hr 20 mins • 12 mins	• 1 kg all-purpose (plain) flour • 650 g water • 200 g liquid sourdough starter • 5 g fresh baker's yeast • 20 g salt	150 g	Bassinage* water added 3 mins before end of kneading.
BAKER'S PEEL (p. 64)	136.4°F (58°C)	480°F (250°C)	• 1 hr 30 mins then 1 hr 30 mins • 18 mins	• 1 kg all-purpose (plain) flour • 650 g water • 200 g liquid sourdough starter • 5 g fresh baker's yeast • 20 g salt	300 g	
PETITE BAGUETTE (p. 66)	136.4°F (58°C)	480°F (250°C)	• 1st resting 1 hr then 1 hr 15 mins and 1 hr 40 mins • 40 mins in dry weather (50 mins in damp weather conditions)	• 1 kg all-purpose (plain) flour • 625 g water • 200 g liquid sourdough starter • 5 g fresh baker's yeast • 20 g salt	460 g	
RUSTIC LOAF (p. 68)	136.4°F (58°C)	480°F (250°C)	• 1 hr 30 mins and 1 hr 30 mins • 25 mins	• 800 g all-purpose (plain) flour • 200 g buckwheat flour • 6 g roasted malt • 620 g water • 200 g liquid sourdough starter • 4 g fresh baker's yeast • 20 g salt	300 g	

Bread	Base Temp.	Oven Temp.	Rising time (1st and 2nd rise) / Baking time	Ingredients	Dough weight per loaf	Comments
TABATIERE (p. 70)	132.8°F (56°C)	480°F (250°C)	• 1st resting 1 hr then 45 mins and 1 hr 30 mins • 24 mins (25 mins in damp weather conditions)	• 1 kg all-purpose (plain) flour • 650 g water • 200 g liquid sourdough starter • 5 g fresh baker's yeast • 20 g salt • Rye flour for dusting	300 g	
SPLIT LOAF (p. 74)	132.8°F (56°C)	480°F (250°C)	• 1st resting 1 hr then 1 hr and 1 hr 20 mins • 20 mins	• 1 kg all-purpose (plain) flour • 650 g water • 200 g liquid sourdough starter • 5 g fresh baker's yeast • 20 g salt	300 g	
DAISY LOAF (p. 76)	132.8°F (56°C)	500°F (260°C)	• 1 hr and 1 hr 30 mins • 6 mins at 500°F (260°C) and 19 mins at 480°F (250°C)	• 900 g all-purpose (plain) flour • 100 g rye flour • 650 g water • 200 g liquid sourdough starter • 4 g fresh baker's yeast • 20 g salt	470 g	Its shape makes it ideal for sharing.
PORTE-MANTEAU (p. 78)	132.8°F (56°C)	480°F (250°C)	• 1st resting 1 hr then 1 hr 30 mins and 1 hr 40 mins • 25 mins	• 1 kg all-purpose (plain) flour • 650 g water • 200 g liquid sourdough starter • 6 g fresh baker's yeast • 20 g salt	300 g	
THE TWIST (p. 82)	132.8°F (56°C)	480°F (250°C)	• 1 hr 30 mins and 1 hr 30 mins • 18 mins	• 1 kg all-purpose (plain) flour • 620 g water • 200 g liquid sourdough starter • 6 g fresh baker's yeast • 20 g salt	300 g	
ZIGZAG BREAD (p. 84)	132.8°F (56°C)	500°F (260°C)	• 1 hr 30 mins and 1 hr 30 mins • 6 mins at 500°F (260°C) and 19 mins at 480°F (250°C)	• 900 g all-purpose (plain) flour • 100 g rye flour, plus extra for dusting • 640 g water • 200 g liquid sourdough starter • 4 g fresh baker's yeast • 20 g salt	550 g	When baked, it has a lovely caramel color.
COURONNE BREAD RING (p. 86)	132.8°F (56°C)	500°F (260°C)	• 1 hr and 1 hr 30 mins • 6 mins at 500°F (260°C) and 15 mins at 480°F (250°C)	• 900 g all-purpose (plain) flour • 100 g rye flour, plus extra for dusting • 650 g water • 200 g liquid sourdough starter • 4 g fresh baker's yeast • 20 g salt	930 g	When baked, it has a lovely caramel color.
BOW TIE BREAD (p. 90)	132.8°F (56°C)	480°F (250°C)	• 2 hrs and 1 hr 20 mins • 6 mins at 500°F (260°C) then 19 mins at 480°F (250°C)	• 900 g all-purpose (plain) flour • 100 g rye flour • 640 g water • 200 g liquid sourdough starter • 4 g fresh baker's yeast • 20 g salt	550 g	When baked, it has a lovely caramel color.

Bread	Base Temp.	Oven Temp.	Rising time (1st and 2nd rise) / Baking time	Ingredients	Dough weight per loaf	Comments
SPECIALTY BREADS						
"FIRST MILL" LOAF (p. 94)	132.8°F (56°C)	482°F (250°C)	• 2 hrs and 2 hrs • 25 mins	• 850 g all-purpose (plain) flour • 100 g "first-mill" flour • 50 g rye flour • 720 g water • 200 g liquid sourdough starter • 2 g fresh baker's yeast • 20 g salt • 20 g grapeseed oil	300 g	With its wheat grain shape, this is a most attractive loaf.
CORNMEAL BREAD (p. 96)	136.4°F (58°C)	480°F (250°C)	• 45 mins and 1 hr 30 mins • 20 mins	• 500 g all-purpose (plain) flour • 500 g cornmeal • 620 g water • 200 g liquid sourdough starter • 6 g fresh baker's yeast • 20 g salt	300 g	Don't over-proof or the dough risks collapsing.
MIXED-SEED BREAD (p. 98)	132.8°F (56°C)	480°F (250°C)	• 1 hr 30 mins and 2 hrs • 20 mins	• 1 kg all-purpose (plain) flour • 600 g water • 200 g liquid sourdough starter • 6 g fresh baker's yeast • 20 g salt • 180 g roasted seeds (flax, poppy seeds, sesame, millet, quinoa), plus extra for topping	300 g	
KAMUT® BREAD (p. 100)	136.4°F (58°C)	480°F (250°C)	• 1 hr and 2 hrs • 25 mins	• 400 g all-purpose (plain) flour • 600 g whole-grain Kamut® flour • 620 g water • 300 g liquid sourdough starter • 4 g fresh baker's yeast • 20 g salt	300 g	The dough can be tricky, so bake in a mold.
WHOLE WHEAT BREAD (p. 104)	132.8°F (56°C)	480°F (250°C)	• 1 hr and 1 hr 30 mins • 25 mins	• 1 kg whole-wheat flour • 720 g water • 200 g liquid sourdough starter • 6 g fresh baker's yeast • 20 g salt	300 g	Choose an organic wholemeal flour and ensure the dough is sufficiently moist.
SEMOLINA BREAD (p. 106)	132.8°F (56°C)	480°F (250°C)	• 2 hrs and 1 hr 30 mins • 20 mins	• 400 g all-purpose (plain) flour • 600 g semolina flour • 650 g water • 200 g liquid sourdough starter • 4 g fresh baker's yeast • 20 g salt	300 g	Place dough on semolina-floured tray for 12 h fermentation at 50°F (10°C).
COUNTRY BREAD (p. 108)	132.8°F (56°C)	500°F (260°C)	• 5 hrs and 1 hr 30 mins • 6 mins at 500°F (260°C) and 19 mins at 464°F (240°C)	• 900 g all-purpose (plain) flour • 100 g rye flour • 680 g water • 200 g liquid sourdough starter • 4 g fresh baker's yeast • 20 g salt	950 g	
BRAN LOAF (p. 110)	132.8°F (56°C)	464°F (240°C)	• 45 mins and 1 hr 30 mins • 25 mins	• 600 g all-purpose (plain) flour • 100 g rye flour • 300 g wheat bran • 640 g water • 200 g liquid sourdough starter • 6 g fresh baker's yeast • 20 g salt	930 g	
RYE BREAD (p. 112)	140°F (60°C)	480°F (250°C)	• 1 hr and 1 hr 30 mins • 30 mins	• 300 g all-purpose (plain) flour • 700 g medium or dark rye flour • 720 g water • 200 g liquid sourdough starter • 3 g fresh baker's yeast • 20 g salt	300 g	
MASLIN LOAF (p. 116)	138.2°F (59°C)	480°F (250°C)	• 1 hr 30 mins and 1 hr 30 mins • 30 mins	• 500 g all-purpose (plain) flour • 500 g medium or dark rye flour • 750 g water • 200 g liquid sourdough starter • 3 g fresh baker's yeast • 20 g salt	300 g	

Bread	Base Temp.	Oven Temp.	Rising time (1st and 2nd rise) / Baking time	Ingredients	Dough weight per loaf	Comments
GLUTEN-FREE CORN BREAD (p. 120)		392°F (200°C)	• 25 mins	• 1 kg fine cornmeal • 660 g milk • 180 g butter • 20 g salt • 240 g egg yolks • 360 g egg whites • 40 g fresh baker's yeast	100 g	
GLUTEN-FREE CHESTNUT FLOUR BREAD (p. 122)		480°F (250°C)	• 25 mins, plus another 10 mins in the turned-off oven	• 800 g chestnut flour • 200 g soy flour • 800 g water • 20 g salt • 10 g (3 teaspoons) fresh baker's yeast	300 g	
ROSEMARY FOCACCIA (p. 124)	132.8°F (56°C)	464°F (240°C)	• 2 hrs and 1 hr 30 mins • 15 mins	• 1 kg all-purpose (plain) flour • 660 g water • 200 g liquid sourdough starter • 14 g fresh baker's yeast • 20 g salt • 60 g olive oil • Fresh rosemary sprigs	940 g	
MACATIA BREAD (p. 128)	132.8°F (56°C)	446°F (230°C)	• 2 hrs and 2 hrs • 15 mins	• 500 g all-purpose (plain) flour • 500 g fine wheat flour (or 1 kg all-purpose [plain] flour) • 450 g water • 200 g liquid sourdough starter • 20 g fresh baker's yeast • 20 g salt • 250 g sugar • 20 g vanilla extract • Peanut oil	490 g	
EKMEK (p. 130)	132.8°F (56°C)	464°F (240°C)	• 1 hr and 2 hrs • 20 mins	• 1 kg all-purpose (plain) flour • 550 g water • 200 g liquid sourdough starter • 3 g fresh baker's yeast • 20 g salt • 80 g olive oil • 150 g clear honey For variations: 200 g dried raspberries and 100 g black sesame seeds	600 g	
PUMPERNICKEL (p. 132)	132.8°F (56°C)	230°F (110°C)	• 1 hr and 16 up to 20h • 6 hrs	• 600 g rye flour • 300 g all-purpose (plain) flour • 100 g precooked bulgur wheat • 1 kg water • 240 g liquid sourdough starter • 20 g salt • 120 g honey • 80 g mixed seeds (anise, coriander, fennel, and caraway seeds) • Butter for greasing	645 kg	
BROA (p. 136)	132.8°F (56°C)	480°F (250°C)	• 1 hr and 1 hr 10 • 25 mins	• 500 g all-purpose (plain) flour • 500 g fine cornmeal • 590 g water • 200 g liquid sourdough starter • 4 g fresh baker's yeast • 20 g salt • 60 g canola (rapeseed) oil	300 g	
BAGELS (p. 138)	132.8°F (56°C)	464°F (240°C)	• 1 hr and 30 mins • 15 mins	• 1 kg all-purpose (plain) flour • 400 g water • 200 g liquid sourdough starter • 10 g fresh baker's yeast • 20 g salt • 40 g sugar • 50 g butter • 2 eggs, plus extra eggs for glazing • Poppy seeds and sesame seeds for the variations	90 g	Bagels are simmered in water for 1 min 30 secs on each side before baking.

Bulk Conversions

Bread	Base Temp.	Oven Temp.	Rising time (1st and 2nd rise) / Baking time	Ingredients	Dough weight per loaf	Comments
SESAME BUNS (p. 142)	132.8°F (56°C)	338°F (170°C)	• 1 hr and 2 hrs • 14 mins	• 1 kg all-purpose (plain) flour • 400 g water • 200 g liquid sourdough starter • 24 g fresh baker's yeast • 20 g salt • 50 g milk powder • 70 g sugar • 100 g softened butter • 150 g egg yolks • 100 g sunflower oil	100 g	
SWISS "CROSS" BREAD (p. 144)	132.8°F (56°C)	500°F (260°C)	• 5 hrs and 1 hr 30 mins • 6 mins at 500°F (260°C) and 19 mins at 480°F (250°C)	• 900 g all-purpose (plain) flour • 100 g rye flour • 640 g water • 200 g liquid sourdough starter • 4 g fresh baker's yeast • 20 g salt	300 g	

Bread	Base Temp.	Oven Temp.	Rising time (1st and 2nd rise) / Baking time	Ingredients	Dough weight per loaf	Comments
ORGANIC NATURALLY-LEAVENED BREADS						
ORGANIC BAGUETTE (p. 148)	136.4°F (58°C)	480°F (250°C)	• 1st resting 1 hr then 1 hr 30 mins and 1 hr 30 mins • 20 mins and 25 mins in damp weather conditions	• 1 kg organic all-purpose (plain) flour • 650 g water • 200 g liquid sourdough starter • 5 g fresh baker's yeast • 20 g salt	300 g	Bassinage* water added 3 mins before end of kneading.
ORGANIC STONE-GROUND BREAD (p. 152)	132.8°F (56°C)	491°F (255°C)	• 1st resting 2 hrs then 2 hrs 45 mins and 2 hrs • 25 mins at 491°F (255°C) then 35 mins at 428°F (220°C)	• 300 g organic all-purpose (plain) flour • 700 g organic stone-ground flour • 700 g water • 510 g liquid sourdough starter • 2 g fresh baker's yeast • 20 g fine sea salt	950 g	
CLASSIC ORGANIC BREAD (p. 154)	136.4°F (58°C)	480°F (250°C)	• 2 hrs and 1 hr 30 mins • 1 hr	• 1 kg organic all-purpose (plain) flour • 500 g water • 200 g liquid sourdough starter • 2 g fresh baker's yeast • 20 g salt	890 kg	
ORGANIC BUCKWHEAT BREAD (p. 158)	132.8°F (56°C)	480°F (250°C)	• 2 hrs and 1 hr 40 mins • 25 mins	• 600 g organic all-purpose (plain) flour • 400 g organic buckwheat flour • 6 g roasted malt (optional) • 600 g water, plus 20 g for 'bassinage' • 200 g liquid sourdough starter • 2 g fresh baker's yeast • 20 g salt	500 g	Bassinage* water added 3 mins before end of kneading.
ORGANIC SPELT BREAD (p. 160)	132.8°F (56°C)	480°F (250°C)	• 1 hr 30 mins and 1 hr 30 mins • 30 mins	• 650 g organic all-purpose (plain) flour • 350 g organic spelt flour • 660 g water • 300 g liquid sourdough starter • 2 g fresh baker's yeast • 20 g salt	400 g	
ORGANIC EINKORN BREAD (p. 164)	138.2°F (56°C)	480°F (250°C)	• 1 hr 30 mins and 1 hr 30 mins • 15 mins at 480°F (250°C) then 30 mins at 428°F (220°C)	• 900 g einkorn flour • 100 g organic all-purpose (plain) flour • 650 g water • 200 g liquid sourdough starter • 2 g fresh baker's yeast • 20 g fine sea salt	1.78 kg	
ORGANIC WHOLE WHEAT BREAD (p. 166)	136.4°F (58°C)	480°F (250°C)	• 1 hr and 1 hr 30 mins • 25 mins	• 1 kg coarse whole wheat flour • 720 g water • 200 g liquid sourdough starter • 2 g fresh baker's yeast • 20 g fine sea salt	300 g	
STONE-GROUND BREAD WITH CURRANTS (p. 168)	136.4°F (58°C)	491°F (255°C)	• 1st resting 2 hrs then 2 hrs 30 mins and 2 hrs • 1 hr	• 1 kg organic stoneground flour • 700 g water • 510 g liquid sourdough starter • 5 g fresh baker's yeast • 20 g salt • 15 % of the dough's weight in currants	950 g	

Bread	Base Temp.	Oven Temp.	Rising time (1st and 2nd rise) / Baking time	Ingredients	Dough weight per loaf	Comments
				BREADS WITH EXTRAS		
HAZELNUT & BUTTER BREAD (p. 172)	132.8°F (56°C)	446°F (230°C)	• 1 hr and 1 hr 15 mins • 20-25 mins	• 500 g all-purpose (plain) flour • 500 g high-gluten wheat flour (or use 1 kg all-purpose flour) • 600 g water • 200 g liquid sourdough starter • 10 g fresh baker's yeast • 20 g salt • 50 g milk powder • 70 g sugar • 100 g butter • 350 g hazelnuts	300 g	
GORGONZOLA & WALNUT BREAD (p. 174)	132.8°F (56°C)	480°F (250°C)	• 1 hr 30 mins and 1 hr 30 mins • 18 mins	• 500 g all-purpose (plain) flour • 500 g fine wheat flour (or 1 kg all-purpose flour) • 650 g water • 200 g liquid sourdough starter • 10 g fresh baker's yeast • 20 g salt • 200 g chopped walnuts • 200 g gorgonzola	300 g	
GREEN TEA & ORANGE LOAF (p. 176)	132.8°F (56°C)	464°F (240°C)	• 2 hrs and 1 hr 15 mins • 20 mins	• 500 g all-purpose (plain) flour • 500 g fine wheat flour (or 1 kg all-purpose flour) • 600 g water • 200 g liquid sourdough starter • 4 g fresh baker's yeast • 20 g salt • 60 g olive oil • 20 g matcha green tea powder • 300 g candied orange peel • 50 g orange-flower water	300 g	
ORANGE BREAD (p. 180)	132.8°F (56°C)	480°F (250°C)	• 2 hrs and 1 hr • 20 mins	• 500 g all-purpose (plain) flour • 500 g fine wheat flour (or 1 kg all-purpose flour) • 620 g water • 200 g liquid sourdough starter • 10 g fresh baker's yeast • 20 g salt • 50 g softened butter • 50 g orange-flower water • 190 g candied orange peel	300 g	
FIG BREAD (p. 182)	132.8°F (56°C)	480°F (250°C)	• 1 hr 30 mins and 1 hr 30 mins • 20 mins	• 500 g all-purpose (plain) flour • 500 g fine wheat flour (or 1 kg all-purpose flour) • 650 g water • 200 g liquid sourdough starter • 10 g fresh baker's yeast • 20 g salt • 400 g dried figs	300 g	
HONEY BREAD (p. 184)	132.8°F (56°C)	392°F (200°C)	• 1 hr 30 mins and 1 hr 30 mins • 20 mins	• 500 g all-purpose (plain) flour • 500 g light rye flour (or 1 kg all-purpose flour) • 500 g water • 200 g liquid sourdough starter • 6 g fresh baker's yeast • 20 g salt • 300 g honey, plus extra for topping	300 g	
WALNUT & BUTTER BREAD (p. 186)	132.8°F (56°C)	446°F (230°C)	• 1 hr 30 mins and 1 hr 15 mins • 17 mins	• 500 g all-purpose (plain) flour • 500 g fine wheat flour (or 1 kg all-purpose (plain) flour) • 450 g water • 200 g liquid sourdough starter • 10 g fresh baker's yeast • 20 g salt • 50 g milk powder • 70 g sugar • 150 g softened butter • 300 g) chopped walnuts	300 g	

Bread	Base Temp.	Oven Temp.	Rising time (1st and 2nd rise) / Baking time	Ingredients	Dough weight per loaf	Comments
TURMERIC BREAD (p. 190)	132.8°F (56°C)	446°F (230°C)	• 1 hr 30 mins and 1 hr • 20-25 mins	• 500 g all-purpose (plain) flour • 500 g fine wheat flour (or 1 kg all-purpose flour) • 600 g water • 200 g liquid sourdough starter • 10 g fresh baker's yeast • 20 g salt • 50 g milk powder • 70 g sugar • 100 g butter • 18 g ground turmeric	300 g	
MIXED FRUIT & NUT CROWNS (p. 192)	132.8°F (56°C)	464°F (240°C)	• 1 hr 30 mins and 1 hr 30 mins • 30 mins	• 500 g all-purpose (plain) flour • 500 g fine wheat flour (or 1 kg all-purpose flour) • 650 g water • 200 g liquid sourdough starter • 10 g fresh baker's yeast • 20 g salt • 30% of the dough's weight in dried fruit and nuts (golden raisins, raisins, dried figs, cranberries or apricots, prunes, hazelnuts, pecans, almonds, cashews, pine nuts, pistachios)	600 g	
SESAME SEED BREAD (p. 196)	132.8°F (56°C)	464°F (240°C)	• 1 hr 30 mins and 1 hr 30 mins • 18 mins	• 500 g all-purpose (plain) flour • 500 g fine wheat flour (or 1 kg all-purpose flour) • 650 g water • 200 g liquid sourdough starter • 10 g fresh baker's yeast • 20 g salt • 200 g roasted sesame seeds, hydrated at 70% • 200 g non-roasted sesame seeds	300 g	
CUTTLEFISH INK BREAD (p. 198)	132.8°F (56°C)	480°F (250°C)	• 20 mins and 25 mins in damp weather conditions	• 1 kg all-purpose (plain) flour • 650 g water • 200 g liquid sourdough starter • 6 g fresh baker's yeast • 20 g salt • 20 g cuttlefish or squid ink	300 g	Bassinage* water added 3 mins before end of kneading.

Bread	Base Temp.	Oven Temp.	Rising time (1st and 2nd rise) / Baking time	Ingredients	Dough weight per loaf	Comments
OIL-ENRICHED BREADS						
PLAIN CIABATTA (p. 202)	132.8°F (56°C)	518°F (270°C)	• 2 hrs and 1 hr • 6 mins at 518°F (270°C) then 9–14 mins at 480°F (250°C)	• 500 g all-purpose (plain) flour • 500 g fine wheat flour (or 1 kg all-purpose (plain) flour) • 680 g water • 200 g liquid sourdough starter • 10 g fresh baker's yeast • 20 g salt • 60 g olive oil, plus extra for brushing	300 g	Don't over-bake. Ciabatta should be a pale cream color.
MIXED SEED CIABATTA (p. 208)	132.8°F (56°C)	518°F (270°C)	• 2 hrs and 1 hr • 6 mins at 518°F (270°C) then 9–14 mins at 480°F (250°C)	• 500 g all-purpose (plain) flour • 500 g fine wheat flour (or 1 kg all-purpose flour) • 680 g water • 200 g liquid sourdough starter • 10 g fresh baker's yeast • 20 g salt • 60 g olive oil, plus extra for brushing • 180 g mixed seeds (millet, pumpkin and sesame) steeped in 200 g water per kg	350 g	Don't over-bake. Ciabatta should be a pale cream color.
BUCKWHEAT CIABATTA (p. 210)	132.8°F (56°C)	518°F (270°C)	• 2 hrs and 1 hr • 6 mins at 518°F (270°C) then 9–14 mins at 480°F (250°C)	• 900 g all-purpose (plain) flour • 100 g buckwheat flour • 700 g water • 200 g liquid sourdough starter • 6 g fresh baker's yeast • 18 g salt • 60 g olive oil, plus extra for brushing	350 g	Don't over-bake. Ciabatta should be a pale cream color.
PUMPKIN SEED CIABATTA (p. 212)	132.8°F (56°C)	518°F (270°C)	• 2 hrs and 1 hr • 6 mins at 518°F (270°C) then 9–14 mins at 480°F (250°C)	• 500 g all-purpose (plain) flour • 500 g fine wheat flour (or 1 kg all-purpose flour) • 680 g water • 200 g liquid sourdough starter • 10 g fresh baker's yeast • 20 g salt • 60 g olive oil, plus extra for brushing • 200 g roasted pumpkin seeds steeped in 200 g water for 1 kg seeds, plus extra	350 g	Don't over-bake. Ciabatta should be a pale cream color.
BASIL BREAD (p. 216)	132.8°F (56°C)	509°F (265°C)	• 2 hrs and 1 hr • 68°F (20°C) to 77°F (25°C)	• 500 g all-purpose (plain) flour • 500 g fine wheat flour (or 1 kg all-purpose plain flour) • 700 g water • 200 g liquid sourdough starter • 6 g fresh baker's yeast • 20 g salt • 60 g olive oil, plus extra for brushing • 150 g basil	350 g	This makes a perfect appetizer, or serve with aperitifs. Don't over-bake. Ciabatta should be a pale cream color.
SUN-DRIED TOMATO BREAD (p. 218)	132.8°F (56°C)	509°F (265°C)	• 2 hrs and 1 hr • 68–77°F (20–25°C)	• 500 g all-purpose (plain) flour • 500 g fine wheat flour (or 1 kg all-purpose (plain) flour) • 700 g water • 200 g liquid sourdough starter • 6 g fresh baker's yeast • 20 g salt • 60 g olive oil, plus extra for brushing • 300 g sun-dried tomatoes	350 g	Don't over-bake. Ciabatta should be a pale cream color.
FOUGASSE WITH ASHE GOAT CHEESE (p. 220)	132.8°F (56°C)	480°F (250°C)	• 2 hrs and 1 hr • 59–68°F (15–20°C)	• 500 g all-purpose (plain) flour • 500 g fine wheat flour (or 1 kg all-purpose [plain] flour) • 680 g water • 200 g liquid sourdough starter • 10 g fresh baker's yeast • 20 g salt • 60 g olive oil, plus extra for brushing • 200 g crème fraîche • 400 g ash goat cheese	350 g	

Bread	Base Temp.	Oven Temp.	Rising time (1st and 2nd rise) / Baking time	Ingredients	Dough weight per loaf	Comments
FOUGASSE WITH BLACK & GREEN OLIVES (p. 222)	132.8°F (56°C)	509°F (265°C)	• 2 hrs and 1 hr • 68-77°F (20-25°C)	• 500 g all-purpose (plain) flour • 500 g fine wheat flour (or 1 kg all-purpose flour) • 700 g water • 200 g liquid sourdough starter • 10 g fresh baker's yeast • 20 g salt • 60 g olive oil, plus extra for brushing • 400 g pitted black and green olives • 200 g grated Emmental	350 g	
FOUGASSE WITH LARDONS (p. 226)	132.8°F (56°C)	509°F (265°C)	• 2 hrs and 1 hr • 68-77°F (20-25°C)	• 500 g all-purpose (plain) flour • 500 g fine wheat flour (or 1 kg all-purpose flour) • 680 g water • 200 g liquid sourdough starter • 10 g fresh baker's yeast • 20 g salt • 60 g olive oil, plus extra for brushing • 200 g crème fraîche • 150 g grated Emmental • 500 g smoked lardons	350 g	
PIZZA (p. 228)	132.8°F (56°C)	480°F (250°C)	• 2 hrs and 1 hr • 59-68°F (15-20°C)	• 500 g all-purpose (plain) flour • 500 g fine wheat flour (or 1 kg all-purpose flour) • 680 g water • 200 g liquid sourdough starter • 10 g fresh baker's yeast • 20 g salt • 60 g olive oil • 30 g superfine (caster) sugar • 400 g fresh tomato sauce • 400 g Emmental • 8 slices of ham	1.8 kg	

Bread	Base Temp.	Oven Temp.	Rising time (1st and 2nd rise) / Baking time	Ingredients	Dough weight per loaf	Comments
				SWEET PASTRIES & BREADS		
PARIS BUNS (p. 234)	132.8°F (56°C)	392°F (200°C)	• 30 mins and 2 hrs • 13-15 mins	• 1 kg all-purpose (plain) flour • 450 g milk • 40 g fresh baker's yeast • 20 g salt • 250 g butter • 70 g superfine (caster) sugar • Eggs for glazing • Pearl sugar for sprinkling	125 g	
VIENNESE BREAD (p. 236)	132.8°F (56°C)	320°F (160°C)	• 30 mins and 1 hr 30 mins • 30-45 mins	• 500 g all-purpose (plain) flour • 500 g fine wheat flour (or 1 kg fine wheat flour) • 450 g water • 150 g liquid sourdough starter • 30 g fresh baker's yeast • 20 g salt • 50 g milk powder • 150 g butter • 70 g sugar • eggs for glazing • 200 g chocolate chips for the variation	190 g	
SUGAR BREAD (p. 240)	132.8°F (56°C)	392°F (200°C)	• 30 mins and 1 hr 30 mins • 25 mins	• 1 kg all-purpose (plain) flour • 300 g water • 200 g liquid sourdough starter • 6 g fresh baker's yeast • 20 g salt • 100 g sugar—sugar syrup made with 100 g sugar and 100 g water • Sunflower oil for oiling	350 g	
CLASSIC BRIOCHE (p. 242)	132.8°F (56°C)	338°F (170°C)	• 2 hrs and 1 hr 30 mins • 25 mins	• 1 kg all-purpose (plain) flour • 600 g eggs • 150 g liquid sourdough starter • 40 g fresh baker's yeast • 20 g salt • 500 g butter • 160 g sugar • 10 g vanilla extract • Eggs for glazing • Pearl sugar • Butter for the molds	300 g	
BRIOCHE LOAF (p. 246)	132.8°F (56°C)	350°F (180°C)	• 30 mins and 1 hr 30 mins • 30 mins	• 1 kg all-purpose (plain) flour • 540 g water • 150 g liquid sourdough starter • 40 g fresh baker's yeast • 20 g salt • 50 g milk powder • 150 g butter • 70 g sugar • Butter for the molds	1 kg	
RAISIN BENOITONS (p. 248)	132.8°F (56°C)	428°F (220°C)	• 1 hr and 1 hr 30 mins • 12-15 mins	• 600 g all-purpose (plain) flour • 400 g rye flour • 720 g water • 150 g liquid sourdough starter • 20 g fresh baker's yeast • 20 g salt • 600 g raisins	80 g	
CROISSANTS (p. 250)	132.8°F (56°C)	338°F (170°C)	• Cooling 4 hrs and proofing 2 hrs • 15 mins	• 1 kg all-purpose (plain) flour • 440 g water • 100 g liquid sourdough starter • 2 eggs • 40 g fresh baker's yeast • 20 g salt • 120 g sugar • 50 g softened butter plus extra 500 g chilled butter • Egg for glazing	60 g	

Bread	Base Temp.	Oven Temp.	Rising time (1st and 2nd rise) / Baking time	Ingredients	Dough weight per loaf	Comments
PAIN AU CHOCOLAT (p. 254)	132.8°F (56°C)	338°F (170°C)	• Cooling 4 hrs and proofing 2 hrs • 15 mins	• 1 kg all-purpose (plain) flour • 440 g water • 100 g liquid sourdough starter • 2 eggs (100 g) • 40 g fresh baker's yeast • 20 g salt • 120 g sugar • 50 g softened butter plus extra 500 g chilled butter • 100 g dark chocolate • Egg for glazing	80 g	
VANILLA ROLLS (p. 258)	132.8°F (56°C)	392°F (200°C)	• 1 hr 10 mins and 1 hr 20 mins • 15 mins	• 1 kg all-purpose (plain) flour • 500 g water • 200 g liquid sourdough starter • 60 g canola (rapeseed) oil • 14 g fresh baker's yeast • 20 g salt • 160 g turbinado sugar • 8 vanilla beans	60 g	
PULLMAN LOAF (p. 260)	132.8°F (56°C)	338°F (170°C)	• 30 mins and 1 hr 30 mins • 30-40 mins	• 1 kg all-purpose (plain) flour • 560 g water • 150 g liquid sourdough starter • 40 g fresh baker's yeast • 20 g salt • 20 g milk powder • 80 g butter • 40 g crème fraîche • 80 g sugar • Eggs for glazing • 80 g pistachio paste for the variation • Butter for the molds	500 g	
PAINS AUX RAISINS (p. 264)	132.8°F (56°C)	338°F (170°C)	• Cooling 4 hrs and proofing 2 hrs • 15 mins	• 1 kg all-purpose (plain) flour • 440 g water • 100 g liquid sourdough starter • 2 eggs (100 g) • 40 g fresh baker's yeast • 20 g salt • 120 g sugar • 50 g softened butter plus extra 500 g • Egg for glazing • Crème pâtissière with 4 eggs, 220 g sugar, 100 g cornstarch, 1 kg milk, 2 vanilla beans • 300 g raisins (15% of the dough's total weight)	80 g	

Bread	Base Temp.	Oven Temp.	Rising time (1st and 2nd rise) / Baking time	Ingredients	Dough weight per loaf	Comments
				BREAD ROLLS		
POPPY SEED ROLLS (p. 270)	132.8°F (56°C)	446°F (230°C)	• 1 hr 30 mins and 1 hr 30 mins/ 12-13 mins	• 1 kg all-purpose (plain) flour • 640 g water • 200 g liquid sourdough starter • 10 g fresh baker's yeast • 20 g salt • 200 g roasted poppy seeds + extra seeds to top the balls	60 g	

BREAD ROLLS WITH LARDONS & PECANS (p. 272)	132.8°F (56°C)	446°F (230°C)	• 1 hr 30 mins and 1 hr 30 mins/ 12-13 mins	• 1 kg all-purpose (plain) flour
				• 620 g water
				• 200 g liquid sourdough starter
				• 10 g fresh baker's yeast
				• 20 g salt
				• 400 g lardons
				  (20% of the dough's total weight)
				• 200 g pecan nuts
				  (10% of the dough's total weight)
					60 g	

PISTOLETS (p. 276)	132.8°F (56°C)	446°F (230°C)	• 1 hr 30 mins and 1 hr 30 mins • 13 mins	• 1 kg all-purpose (plain) flour • 620 g water • 200 g liquid sourdough starter • 6 g fresh baker's yeast • 20 g salt	75 g	
KAMUT® & SEAWEED BREAD ROLLS (p. 278)	132.8°F (56°C)	437°F (225°C)	• 30 mins and 2 hrs • 12-13 mins	• 400 g all-purpose (plain) flour • 600 g whole-grain Kamut® flour • 600 g water • 300 g liquid sourdough starter • 4 g fresh baker's yeast • 20 g salt • 180 g dried seaweed	50-60 g	

HAZELNUT & CHOCOLATE ROLLS (p. 280)	132.8°F (56°C)	392°F (200°C)	• 1 hr and 1 hr 15 mins
			• 15 mins
				• 1 kg all-purpose (plain) flour
				• 550 g water
				• 200 g liquid sourdough starter
				• 14 g fresh baker's yeast
				• 20 g salt
				• 50 g milk powder
				• 70 g sugar
				• 150 g softened butter
				• Eggs for glazing
				• 180 g hazelnuts
				  (10% of the dough's total weight)
				• 180 g dark chocolate
				  (10% of the dough's total weight)
					125 g	

BREAKFAST ROLLS WITH WALNUTS & RAISINS (p. 284)	132.8°F (56°C)	446°F (230°C)	• 1 hr and 1 hr 30 mins • 15-20 mins	• 500 g all-purpose (plain) flour • 500 g rye flour • 700 g water • 200 g liquid sourdough starter • 6 g fresh baker's yeast • 20 g salt • 200 g walnut halves • 200 g raisins (combined nuts and fruit = 10% of the dough's total weight)	180 g	
BREADSTICKS (p. 286)	132.8°F (56°C)	446°F (230°C)	• 1 hr and 45 mins • 9 mins	• 1 kg all-purpose (plain) flour • 450 g water • 100 g liquid sourdough starter • 10 g fresh baker's yeast • 20 g salt • 150 g olive oil	60 g	

CONVERSIONS

WEIGHT

10 g	—	¼ oz
20 g	—	½ oz
25 g	—	1 oz
50 g	—	2 oz
60 g	—	2½ oz
75 g	—	3 oz
100 g	—	3½ oz
110 g	—	4 oz
150 g	—	5 oz
175 g	—	6 oz
200 g	—	7 oz
225 g	—	8 oz
250 g	—	9 oz
275 g	—	10 oz
350 g	—	12 oz
400 g	—	14 oz
450 g	—	1 lb
500 g	—	18 oz
600 g	—	1¼ lb
700 g	—	1½ lb
900 g	—	2 lb
1 kg	—	2¼ lb
1.1 kg	—	2½ lb
1.3 kg	—	3 lb
1.5 kg	—	3 lb 5 oz
1.6 kg	—	3½ lb
1.8 kg	—	4 lb
2 kg	—	4½ lb
2.2 kg	—	5 lb

VOLUMES

5 ml	—	1 teaspoon
10 ml	—	1 dessert spoon
15 ml	—	1 tablespoon
30 ml	—	1 fl oz
50 ml	—	2 fl oz
75 ml	—	3 fl oz
100 ml	—	3½ fl oz
125 ml	—	4 fl oz (½ pt)
150 ml	—	5 fl oz (¼ pt)
200 ml	—	7 fl oz (⅓ pt)
250 ml	—	9 fl oz
300 ml	—	10 fl oz (½ pt)
350 ml	—	12 fl oz
400 ml	—	14 fl oz
425 ml	—	15 fl oz
450 ml	—	16 fl oz
500 ml	—	18 fl oz
600 ml	—	20 fl oz (1 pt)
700 ml	—	1¼ pints
850 ml	—	1½ pints
1 liter	—	1¾ pints
1.2 liters	—	2 pints
1.5 liters	—	2½ pints
1.8 liters	—	3 pints
2 liters	—	3½ pints

MEASUREMENTS

3 mm	—	⅛ inch
5 mm	—	¼ inch
1 cm	—	½ inch
2 cm	—	¾ inch
2.5 cm	—	1 inch
3 cm	—	1¼ inches
4 cm	—	1½ inches
5 cm	—	2 inches
6 cm	—	2¼ inches
7.5 cm	—	2½ inches
9 cm	—	3 inches
10 cm	—	3½ inches
11.5 cm	—	4½ inches
12.5 cm	—	5 inches
15 cm	—	6 inches
17 cm	—	6½ inches
18 cm	—	7 inches
20.5 cm	—	8 inches
23 cm	—	9 inches
24 cm	—	9½ inches
25.5 cm	—	10 inches
30.5 cm	—	11 inches

FLOURS

All-purpose (plain) flour	—	*Farine de blé T65*
Organic all-purpose (plain) flour	—	*Farine de blé T65 bio*
Organic stone-ground fllour	—	*Farine de meule T65 bio*
Organic flour for rolls or baguettes	—	*Farine de blé T80*
Organic fine stone-ground flour	—	*Farine de meule T80 bio*
Whole wheat flour	—	*Farine de blé T110*
Coarse whole wheat flour	—	*Farine de blé T150*
Coarse, organic whole wheat flour	—	*Farine de blé T150 bio*
Light rye flour	—	*Farine de seigle T80*
Medium rye flour	—	*Farine de seigle T130*
Dark rye flour	—	*Farine de seigle T170*
Buckwheat flour	—	*Farine de sarrasin*
Fine cornmeal flour	—	*Farine de mais*
Fine semolina flour	—	*Semoule de blé*
Wheat bran	—	*Son de blé*
Chestnut flour	—	*Farine de chataigne*
Soya flour	—	*Farine de soya*
Spelt flour	—	*Farine d'épautre*
Einkorn flour	—	*Farine d'engrain (bio)*

TEMPERATURES

F°	C°	Gas	Description
225	110	¼	Very cool
250	130	½	—
275	140	1	cool
300	150	2	—
325	170	3	very moderate
350	180	4	moderate
375	190	5	—
400	200	6	moderately hot
425	220	7	hot
450	230	8	—
475	240	9	very hot

GLOSSARY

Words with an asterisk* are explained within this glossary.

AMYLASE
A natural enzyme found in flour that breaks down starch into fermentable sugars. These are then mainly converted into carbon dioxide (CO_2) and alcohol during fermentation*.

ASH CONTENT
This is a European method used to determine a flour's type (``T'' grade). It represents the mineral residue left after flour is burnt at a temperature of 1652°F (900°C). The higher the T grade, the more husks (bran*) are present in the flour, making it more ``complete.''

BAKER'S LAME
A razor-sharp baker's knife, usually mounted on a special handle, used to score* dough prior to baking.

BAKER'S PEEL
A wooden paddle used to slide dough—especially flatbreads and pizzas—into the oven.

BAKER'S YEAST
A single-celled micro-organism (*Saccharomyces cerevisiae*) used to leaven bread. It is capable of reproducing and multiplying very rapidly in sugar-rich environments, converting sugars into carbon dioxide, which makes the dough rise.

BANNETON
A wicker proofing basket, usually lined with heavy linen. Used for proofing*, particularly for very wet doughs.

BASE TEMPERATURE
Used to calculate the temperature of dough after kneading, usually 75-77°F (24-25°C), by adding the ambient (room) temperature to the temperature of the flour and water.

BASSINAGE
A process whereby a quantity of water is held in reserve and then added at the end of kneading to loosen a very stiff dough.

BATARD
A torpedo-shaped loaf, shorter than a baguette, but not as round as the old-style *pain de deux livres*.

BOULER
To shape dough into balls. The French *boule* (round loaf) gets its name from this word.

BRAN
The outer husk or hull of cereals, which can be removed or retained during grinding. The bran contains the bulk of a grain's fiber.

COUCHE
Heavy-weight linen fabric (also known as a baker's cloth) used for proofing*. Folds in the cloth keep the pieces of dough separate and prevent them from touching.

CRUMB
A term used to define the inside of the bread. By looking at the cell structure of the crumb, bakers can analyze the hydration, flour types, and yeast amounts.

DEFLATE
To release air from the dough during the first fermentation (first rise). This is achieved by folding the dough over on itself. It helps strengthen the gluten structure and helps the dough rise more effectively during the second fermentation* (proofing*).

FERMENTATION
An organic chemical activity whereby sugars contained in the flour are transformed in an anaerobic environment (without air) through the action of yeasts and enzymes (see amylase*). In baking, the fermentation is ``alcoholic,'' in that the simple sugars (glucose, maltose) are broken down by yeasts into carbon dioxide and ethyl alcohol. Carbon

dioxide causes the dough to rise. The fermentation comprises two stages: first rise* after kneading, and proofing* after shaping.

FIRST RESTING
Also known as *autolyse*, this is a pre-fermentation resting period, prior to kneading. This process helps the gluten* develop more quickly, gives a more elastic dough, and reduces the length of kneading time.

FIRST RISE
The first period of fermentation* that begins after kneading but before the dough is divided into pieces and shaped*. It is done at room temperature in a draft-free spot and can include a period in the refrigerator.

GLAZE
To create a glossy appearance on the surface of a bread. Often achieved by brushing the dough with a lightly beaten egg just prior to baking.

GLUTEN
The elastic matter formed in dough by the proteins (mainly gliadins and glutenins), when kneaded with liquid. Found in nearly all cereals used for bread. Kneading* develops the glutens into strands that form a glutinaceous network. These contain the carbon dioxide that expands during the fermentation and subsequent baking.

HYDRATION
The ratio of water to flour in a given recipe.

KNEAD
The process of working a dough, by hand or in a stand mixer, to evenly blend the ingredients and to develop the gluten. Kneading* by hand involves pushing and pulling the dough on a work surface, turning it and shaping* it to aerate the dough and help it form a glutinaceous network. As the structure changes, the dough becomes smoother and more elastic.

LEAVEN
To incorporate a rising agent—natural starter, yeast, baking powder, etc.—into a dough to make it ferment and rise. Natural leavens, such as sourdough starters, use natural "wild" yeasts in the dough to start the fermentation*.

POOLISH
A pre-ferment (starter) made with a mix of equal parts of water and flour. Used in conjunction with fresh baker's yeast.

PROOF/PROOFING TIME
Known as *l'apprêt*, this is the second stage of fermentation, which begins after the dough has been portioned and shaped, and continues until it is put in the oven. It is done at room temperature in a draft-free spot.

REFRESH
To keep a natural starter alive by feeding it with flour and water.

REST
To set a dough aside after kneading* or working. This allows the gluten,* which will tighten as the dough is worked, to relax.

SCORING
The process of making shallow cuts or slashes, in various designs, along the surface of the dough. Usually done just prior to baking. Scoring helps to control the way the bread rises as it bakes.

SEAM
The point at which the edges of the dough—both in a ball and a long shape—meet to form a closure, or seam.

SHAPING
The process which gives the dough its form. Often done in two stages, but it is the second, more precise shaping, that creates the final appearance of the baked loaf.

SIMMER
To cook in liquid just below the boiling point, around 208°F (98°C). Small bubbles rise through the liquid and break the surface.

STALE
Over time, moisture is gradually lost from bread and it becomes stale. As it does so, the bread becomes hard and both aroma and flavor deteriorate.

STEAM INJECTION
A process of introducing water into an oven to create steam as the dough goes in to bake. This is achieved by splashing water onto a preheated baking sheet.

STEEP
To immerse and soak seeds or fruit (usually dried) in a liquid to soften and rehydrate them.

TOURAGE
A term used in French patisserie, whereby butter is rolled out and folded into a dough to enrich and lighten the texture as it bakes.

WELL
A large hollow created in the center of a mound of flour (on a work surface or in a bowl) to contain liquid ingredients. The dry ingredients are gradually worked into the liquid, so as to create a smooth, well-blended paste.

Index

Phaidon Press Limited
Regent's Wharf
All Saints Street
London N1 9PA

Phaidon Press Inc.
65 Bleecker Street
New York, NY 10012

www.phaidon.com

© 2015 Phaidon Press Limited

ISBN: 978 07148 6887 5

The Larousse Book of Bread
originates from *Le Larousse du Pain*
by Éric Kayser, © Larousse 2013

A CIP catalogue record
for this book is available
from the British Library.

Commissioning Editor: Emilia Terragni
Project Editor: Michelle Lo
Production Controller: Leonie Kellman

Design by Sarah Boris
Layout by Frédéric Tacer
Photographs by Massimo Pessina

Translations by JMS Books, LLP

Printed in China

The publisher would like to thank
Éric Kayser, Jean-Francois Richez,
Isabelle Poullalie, Cindi Kruth, Lucy
Malouf, and Marisa Robertson-Textor
for their contributions to the book.

RECIPE NOTES

Butter should always
be unsalted.

Pepper is always freshly ground
black pepper, unless otherwise
specified.

Eggs, vegetables, and fruits
are assumed to be large size,
unless otherwise specified.
For UK, use medium eggs.

Milk is always whole,
unless otherwise specified.

Ham means cooked ham,
unless otherwise specified.

Cooking and preparation times
are for guidance only,
as individual ovens vary.
If using a fan oven, follow the
manufacturer's instructions
concerning oven temperatures.

The author and publisher
strongly advise to work
with weight measurements
for precise results.

When measuring flour by
cups, whisk the flour before
measuring.

All salt should be flaky sea salt.